Praise for *Real Estate on Your Terms*

"I've known Chris for over 20 years as a business associate, client, and friend. I've seen his struggles and successes, his victories and defeats. Most importantly I have seen him grow as a person, a husband, a father, a friend, and a businessperson. His remarkable rebound story is an example of what can be accomplished when you have the will to win, the courage to be your best, and the honesty to truly assess your position in life . . . and then go out and do something about it!

Most importantly, Chris walks the talk. He is accountable, disciplined, and remarkably resilient. Whether you are seeking guidance in the real estate sales arena as a facilitator or as an investor, there is no better guide for you than Chris Prefontaine. All you have to do is look up the definition of 'champion' in the dictionary; that's where you will find what Chris epitomizes and what you will become when you work with him."

—John Alexandrov, attorney, international best-selling author, coach

"If you want a coach/mentor who is talking the talk and walking the walk, Chris is definitely the guy. Not only does he have a ton of experience but he doesn't hold back any punches, and he provides the evidence to support his success. I strongly recommend Chris and his team if you are still on the fence. Invest in yourself and a good coach and mentor. Thanks, Chris."

—Sergio Ortega, owner, Real Property Solvers

"Chris Prefontaine knows, and for that matter, so does the entire Prefontaine family, what it means to do the work that has to be done to reach the goal. Unlike other 'successful' people who pull up the ladder when they 'get theirs,' Chris measures success by how high he can elevate everyone around him by sharing what he has learned."

—Jay F. Theise, Esq.

"Chris Prefontaine is an amazing entrepreneur and a man for which I have tremendous respect. I have had the pleasure of working with him over the past fifteen years. He is a man of integrity, and he seeks to help others and build relationships that last. This book is eye opening, and Chris describes what he knows best ... teaching others how to win. I highly recommend this book and hope that you will take his lesson and message to heart."

—Joseph Land, JL Capital Group, LLC

"I've known Chris Prefontaine since grade school. He knows his stuff and has a knack for encouraging while educating people. He was a mentor to me and helped increase my residual income."

—Darren LaCroix, CSP, AS, 2001 World Champion of Public Speaking

"Chris has been a client and friend for close to 20 years and a business partner for ten years. We own a building in Illinois together. I'm also an investor of Chris's all stemming from him coming to interview our law firm when he moved to the area in 2004. One of the most disciplined and hardest working people I know, he is the ultimate entrepreneur. The advice in his book comes from years of hard-won, practical experience. Pay attention and never give up."

—Richard Sayer, Esq., Sayer Regan & Thayer, Newport, RI

"Real Estate on Your Terms is filled with practical, workable methods for anyone wanting to build consistent sustainable cash flow and long-term wealth. Chris Prefontaine lays out a simple plan and implements a specific system that, when put into action, will be very profitable for novice and experienced investors alike.

I've experienced firsthand the value of Chris's methods in action through his mentoring and closing highly profitable deals. If you're looking for results, Real Estate on Your Terms *is packed full of proven techniques and I would encourage anyone looking for financial freedom to read Chris's book."*

—Don Strickland, Owner, Structure Property Solutions

"An outstanding resource for anyone who wants to have success in the world of real estate investing and move onward to that next level. Chris shares his real-world perspectives gained from over 25 years of experience as a practitioner, investor, and industry expert. Chris has coached more than 30,000 people and has been part of $75 million worth of deals. And now in this book, Chris masterfully dissects the nine steps you need in order to become your own master transaction engineer. This is quite a master-piece and is well needed in the marketplace. You will do deals after reading Chris's book."

—Stephen Woessner, CEO of Predictive ROI and host of the top-rated Onward Nation podcast

"In his book Chris tells a compelling story on how to invest in real estate with less risk and better cash flow than the conventional process of buy and hold or property flips. If, like many, you are concerned with the risks of investing in the stock market or regular real estate, this book could change your perspective—a worthy read.

—Paul Dion, CPA, CTC, www.smarttaxadvisor.com

"Whenever you can learn from mistakes, hardships, and tragedies of others, you might want to take notes. In Chris Pre-fontaine's book, Real Estate on Your Terms, *it is an opportunity to advance. From 'lease options' to 'forced profits' the strategies in this book are quite capable of setting one free. The question is, what do you do when life happens? Chris is a fine example of persistence and resilience. We can all stand a refresher course in that. I highly recommend you read* Real Estate on your Terms. *"*

—Mitch Stephen, Founder of 1000houses.com and podcast host of reinvestorsummit.com

"Starting new ventures is filled with deep potholes and stormy economic markets; a wise man finds a guide to help. Not to worry, here is a guy to guide and nurture you step by step. Chris Prefontaine is a business builder and entrepreneur. As a coach and mentor, he is superior. Chris not only builds businesses but he also knows how to sell and make profits and then move onto bigger and better deals.

Chris is that rare one-in-a-million person who knows 'the success formula' that you, the reader, want and need. In this text Chris does not hold back; he reveals all the information that you are searching for. He exposes his systems and formulas clearly

in a way the average person will understand. Chris will save you hours of frustration and show you how to avoid the pain of making big decisions and he'll do that by following a proven and tested system. His system will result in large profits for you.

Next, you need to find a comfortable chair, shut off your computer and telephone, and let your guide train and show you how to be successful in a unique business. Chris is no ivory tower professor from the university; this is a guy that comes from the trenches of work. Expect no hype, just great business stuff that will get you to the bank with deposits. In a simple chapter after chapter, planned process, Chris is going to transform, teach, guide, and nurture you through his formula of special success. Chris has created a proven, successful, moneymaking program. You'll be learning from a professional, and your small investment in time will bring you astonishing rewards."

—Ted Thomas, tax lien certificate and tax deed authority, www.tedthomas.com

"I've known Chris since freshman year of college when he used to go home on weekends to work in his family business. He was unbelievably focused and disciplined at age 18, balancing work, spending time with Kim, and getting his schoolwork done. He was like a 30-year-old businessman living amongst a bunch of partying college kids. He hasn't changed. He is the most driven and focused person I know! If you are interested in any aspect of the real estate business I would highly recommend working with and learning from Chris. Learn from his tremendous knowledge and experience and put yourself in the best position to succeed!"

—Robert E. Romano, estate planning attorney and real estate investor

REAL ESTATE
ON
your terms

CHRIS PREFONTAINE

REAL ESTATE ON *your terms*

CREATE CONTINUOUS CASH FLOW NOW,
WITHOUT USING YOUR CASH OR CREDIT

Advantage.

Published by Advantage, Charleston, South Carolina.
Member of Advantage Media Group.

ADVANTAGE is a registered trademark, and the Advantage colophon is a trademark of Advantage Media Group, Inc.

Printed in the United States of America.

10 9 8 7 6 5 4 3 2 1

ISBN: 978-1-59932-819-5
LCCN: 2017936766

Cover design by Katie Biondo.

This publication is designed to provide accurate and authoritative information in regard to the subject matter covered. It is sold with the understanding that the publisher is not engaged in rendering legal, accounting, or other professional services. If legal advice or other expert assistance is required, the services of a competent professional person should be sought.

Advantage Media Group is proud to be a part of the Tree Neutral® program. Tree Neutral offsets the number of trees consumed in the production and printing of this book by taking proactive steps such as planting trees in direct proportion to the number of trees used to print books. To learn more about Tree Neutral, please visit **www.treeneutral.com.**

Advantage Media Group is a publisher of business, self-improvement, and professional development books. We help entrepreneurs, business leaders, and professionals share their Stories, Passion, and Knowledge to help others Learn & Grow. Do you have a manuscript or book idea that you would like us to consider for publishing? Please visit **advantagefamily.com** or call **1.866.775.1696.**

To my wife, Kim, for sticking with me through all the ups and downs, the goods and bads. It is certainly true that behind every good man is an amazing wife. I couldn't have done it without her. Heck, she has stuck with me for 31 years as of the writing of this book!

To my son, Nick, who watched firsthand through the 2008–2012 transition, and to my daughter, Kayla, and Kayla's husband, Zach, who joined the biz in 2016. As of the writing of this book, they have grown into pivotal roles and are more than capable of running the entire business for the many decades ahead.

table of contents

FOREWORD BY RON LEGRAND xv

FOREWORD BY SCOTT ULMER xix

ACKNOWLEDGMENTS xxi

ABOUT THE AUTHOR xxiii

INTRODUCTION 1
My 2008 Debacle Is Yours to Learn From

CHAPTER 1 15
On YOUR TERMS—What That Means

CHAPTER 2 25
Yeah, but (Fill In Your Self-Imposed Roadblock Here)

CHAPTER 3 43
*Nine Steps to Becoming a Master
Transaction Engineer*

CHAPTER 4 65
You Can Make All the Difference

CHAPTER 5 79
The Path to Profits: Knowing What Deal Type to Use

CHAPTER 6 97
Okay, I Have These Properties, Now What Do I Do?

CHAPTER 7 111
Simple, Proven, Predictable, and
Profitable with the Right Coach

CHAPTER 8 127
What Could Go Wrong?

CHAPTER 9 133
Design Your Lifestyle

CONCLUSION 147

APPENDIX 149

foreword

by Ron LeGrand

Chris Prefontaine was already a successful businessman when he showed up at one of my real estate seminars around 2005, a meeting that has been exceptionally rewarding for both of us through the ensuing years.

I have been traveling all over the country for more than two decades putting on "millionaire-maker" workshops sharing my own hard-learned lessons on how to buy real estate without risking your money and credit. All kinds of people attend these seminars, but many show up because their fortunes have fallen short of their dreams. They feel they are working too hard, earning too little, and not spending enough time with their families. Chris was different.

He was working hard but always understood the need to put his family first. Chris and his wife, Kim, worked together building and rehabbing homes, and then he created and sold a successful real estate brokerage. He understood how to apply his knowledge of real estate to create multiple income streams as an investor, developer, marketer, and coach. Some seminar leaders might be intimidated to have someone in the audience as knowledgeable and assertive as Chris, but I found his presence inspiring.

Even more inspiring, Chris engineered a successful comeback from devastating losses in the 2008 collapse of the real estate market. He unsparingly details in this book how that experience affected him and his family. You will wonder how he got the strength to do what he did, and he'll tell you an intensely personal story that answers your question.

Chris has been returning every year to at least one of my events, and he participates in my high-level mastermind group, which allows entrepreneurs like him to tap their peers for sometimes life-changing ideas. Chris embraced my philosophy that we can all benefit at every stage from mentoring and constructive criticism, from coaching in all aspects of our personal and business lives. Now if you read this book, you will benefit from the combined life lessons of Chris, his mentors like me, and our fellow masterminds. You'll learn how to stop wasting time on bad habits and menial tasks, how to be more disciplined and systematic—business basics that are ignored by too many authors of books like this.

In this book, Chris lays out a real estate investment philosophy that is in his words "simple, proven, predictable, and profitable." He speaks from experience because he personally is in the trenches every day, doing real deals. I know this claim is true because I have partnered with Chris or coached him on some of his biggest deals. The course Chris lays out for you is one I have taken, vouch for, and recommend.

In my own recent book I explain how you can use automation, outsourcing, and delegation *in* your business to make more time to work *on* your business, improving it and providing a more rewarding lifestyle for you and your family. Guess who is a walking advertisement for the benefits of applying that approach? Chris has grown his business from a regional dealmaker into a national force in his real estate transaction niche by expertly managing his time. In the process he has created rewarding careers for three family members and provided jobs to various assistants while still having time for his personal needs, including real vacations. Chris makes—to borrow a real estate term—the highest and best use of his time. And he shows you in this book exactly how he does it.

Chris provides a step-by-step guide, and unlike some authors, he is not afraid to be candid about what can go wrong. That's because he's writing not just as an expert but also as a guide and mentor who is willing to take his readers on as students and eventually business partners. If you realize after reading this book that you want to tap into Chris's systems and benefit from his coaching, my advice is to waste no time doing so. Chris is so successful at what he does that he may be camped out on a Caribbean island some day enjoying the good life.

—Ron LeGrand, author of *How to Be a Quick-Turn Real Estate Millionaire*

by Scott Ulmer

Ever driven down a country road, glanced over, and noticed, in the middle of a crowded cornfield, one stalk sticking out above the rest? Every once in a while, someone crosses your path who catches your eye and grabs your attention—who "sticks out" from the crowd and, for reasons you are not quite sure of at first, leaves a lasting imprint on you. Whatever "it" is, they seem to have it. Their qualities and characteristics leave you without a glimmer of doubt that they are destined to achieve great success in whatever their endeavor.

It was in 2013 that Chris Prefontaine and I crossed paths. I had the distinct pleasure of working with him as he and countless others rebuilt the lives and financial success they had prior to the devastation the 2008 market crash brought.

It was clear from the outset that Chris stuck out above the rest. His sense of focus and purpose-driven approach to life, combined with his Rhode Island twang, made it a pleasure to connect with him every week. And to see the success he achieved in such a short time was a true pleasure for me.

I was coaching several seasoned real estate pros all over the country at the time, figuring out how to navigate the new real estate world. Chris was head and shoulders beyond anyone else I had coached prior to that time and still to this day. It was evident he was a superstar from the first time we ever chatted. He epitomized everything a high-level performer has, and in no time at all he was back to crushing his real estate deals, rebuilding the empire he had once built before, only this time he would build it stronger and battle hardened.

Even though I was supposed to be the one coaching Chris, the truth is, I got as much from our calls each week as he did. To this day I consider him a friend, and every time we talk I glean another "nugget of gold" from him. But for Chris it wasn't just "rising from the proverbial ashes"; he was on a mission to provide for his wife and family—to get them back the lives they had and deserved to have again.

Since that time I have had a front-row seat to his rocket ship rise back to the top. I have watched him crush the goals he set and exceed far above even his tremendously high expectations. And now you too, the reader, have the privilege and pleasure of seeing Chris's off-the-charts comeback and the circumstances and obstacles he overcame to get there, achieving greater and fuller success than he had before.

You will hear firsthand Chris's story of restoration and the personal challenges he had to deal with in the midst of his rebuild; how he is a *master* at nontraditional and creative real estate deals; and how you too can emulate his success if you are tenacious and willing to put in the work, simply by following the outline he provides in this book.

Nothing in life worth having comes easy, but if you are willing to put in the time and follow directions, the following pages will outline step-by-step Chris's blueprint for success in real estate in today's market. You will enjoy not only hearing Chris's story but the valuable content contained within. Whether a seasoned real estate pro or a beginner, I promise you will have several takeaways from this insightful book.

And be sure you have a highlighter and pen close by, as your mind will be stimulated with ideas and inspiration to go out and create the life and success you deserve for you and your family.

—Scott Ulmer
Jacksonville, Florida

acknowledgments

This book could not have been written without the help, influence, and inspiration of many people. It's simply not possible to thank everyone who contributes to a project of this scope, but I'd like to make special mention of a few people.

First and foremost, I'd like to thank my wife, Kim, for the amazing support, encouragement, inspiration, and work on this project. The early mornings and late nights would not be possible without that very important sounding board and unending support.

Second, my kids, who are now not only an integral part of our businesses but helped with this project each step of the way: son Nick, daughter Kayla, and son-in-law Zach. I know you guys will be writing your own books in the near future and I am enjoying watching your growth.

I'd also like to express my appreciation and admiration for one of my main mentors over the years—Ron Legrand. Ron has given me ideas not just for this book but for business in general that have translated into hundreds of thousands of dollars directly. Ron, I'm forever grateful.

I'd also like to express my appreciation to my parents—Bob and Lin—for their continued support with the book and everything else that I journey off to accomplish, as well as my late brother Jay who passed away at the young age of 47 and who was a writer who helped mold my writing style and habits by his never-ending editing of e-books and stories over the years. Jay, we may have never gotten the chance to write together, but your inspiration served the book very well.

Special thanks must also go to one of my attorneys who's also my friend, Richard Sayer. Richard stood by me and encouraged me and believed in me even during the downturn.

Special thanks to my friend and coach early on in my transition time, Scott Ulmer.

I must also express my tremendous appreciation to Advantage Media and their numerous staff people who made this project a reality. A project of this size is made much less difficult with their kind of assistance.

Chris Prefontaine has had multiple careers within the real estate industry over more than 25 years. He built more than a hundred single-family homes in the 1990s. From 1994–2000, he owned a Realty Executives franchise in Massachusetts before selling his real estate brokerage to Coldwell Banker. He; his wife, Kim; and his business partners have converted numerous multifamily homes into condominiums and converted single-family ranch homes into colonials in growth neighborhoods ("raise the roof" projects).

Chris has a passion for continuous education and helping others grow to their full potential. He has coached more than 30,000 people throughout the United States and Canada since the year 2000. He has participated annually in Ron LeGrand's high-end mastermind group. Chris's company, Pre Property Solutions, emerged from a financial debacle in 2008, an amazing turnaround that Chris explains in this book. The family business in Newport, Rhode Island, buys four to ten properties per month, mostly via lease-purchases, and has engineered more than $75 million worth of real estate transactions. The company also coaches and does deals with Joint-Venture Partners around the country.

MY 2008 DEBACLE IS YOURS TO LEARN FROM

Kim and I were sitting at our kitchen island in one of our homes, in Shrewsbury, Massachusetts. Our kids were in the next room, Kayla doing her homework and Nick studying his real estate material. It was February 2008, but looking back I still vividly remember that night—I'll never forget it. Kim and I were just getting ready for dinner, and I could smell the awesome Italian meal cooking on the stove. The cars in the driveway were all brand new, as was the home. Everything was perfect, or so it appeared. But if you saw the look on my face you would know that something was up.

You would have heard Kim say to me, "Okay, we just did the refinance; a couple hundred thousand dollars came in and out—like that. What are we going to do next month? The overall real estate market is crashing—how are we going to do this?"

We were responsible for hundreds of subcontractors and a dozen employees. We had had some amazingly profitable years together and owned 23 properties, some with partner-investors. The properties were all either in foreclosure, going through the foreclosure process, or in a short sale. It was a full-time job just to handle that. We had the IRS calling and sending nastygrams. Our credit cards had been shut off, sometimes without notice. Eight to ten years' worth of savings, investments, college funds, and retirement funds had been cashed out to try to survive.

I said to Kim, "What the heck were we thinking?"

Our daughter, Kayla, was 18, finishing up in a private high school and looking forward to college. Our son, Nick, was 19. Refinancing our second home in Newport, Rhode Island, on two acres overlooking the harbor was supposed to have provided enough cash ($350,000) to save our real estate company. But we had a couple of million dollars in mortgages on top of our children's education expenses. I had made the ultimate mistake of thinking the housing market was never going to stop climbing. Too many of us used our real estate holdings like an ATM machine. The cash-out we had gotten from the refinancing was a bandage that allowed us to pay expenses for our businesses temporarily but required another round of refinancing at a lower interest rate within 12 months.

Chest pains were constant with all that stress. You know how the real estate market came to a halt in 2007–2008. Property values plunged leading to the drying up of credit. Then, in February 2008, almost like a light switch was thrown, financing stopped. Deal funding stopped. All large commercial deals on the books and projected to provide hundreds of thousands of profit were dead in the water with all banks shutting down funding.

Clearly this was not real estate on *my* terms but rather on the banks' terms.

Financing at the time was a challenge because I had purchased buildings the conventional way—putting 10 percent or 20 percent of our money or investors' money down and signing for a loan. The goal pre-2007 had been to accumulate 20 or so properties using cash, investors, and bank loans. Then as the market continued to rise and as we improved the properties, the plan was to sell those off at a profit. That was no longer a path to get out when market values fell by one-third to one-half in 2007. We had no safeguard against a market crash nor did we really create any up-front or ongoing cash flow—we were focused on long-term wealth and cash-outs only. (You'll see in this book how we fixed our business's cash flow challenge by creating the **Three Paydays**.)

Before the real estate market crash, about one-third of our purchases were **commercial or mixed-use properties** and the rest were two- to six-unit apartment buildings, half of which could become condominiums. We would work with engineers and attorneys to completely rehabilitate all of the units of those multifamily buildings, convert them into condos, and resell at a nice profit, usually within a few months. The profit was fantastic until the downturn, when we got caught with four or five units that we had to rent or sell at a loss.

THREE PAYDAYS:

1. A cash deposit from the down payment
2. Monthly cash flow
3. Back-end profit

COMMERCIAL PROPERTIES:

Buildings or land intended to generate a profit.

MIXED-USE PROPERTIES:

Building or complex that blends residential, commercial, and other property types together.

An example of one that got caught in the crash: My business partners and I bought a six-unit apartment building for $500,000 to convert into condos. We put $250,000 into the rehab in an area in Providence with several nearby colleges and were able to sell three units at $172,000 apiece. Six months later, after the crash, we could not get $70,000, and the last two went a year later for less

3

than $50,000 each. That left us underwater on the building purchase, plus interest and the construction costs.

The mixed-use buildings had similar problems. One in Rhode Island, in a lower- to middle-class inner-city area, had four retail units, with four residential units above. I brought in an investor for about $200,000 but still had a $500,000 bank loan. The four commercial units—a nail salon, a beauty parlor, an office, and a window and siding retailer—were supposed to provide most of the income, but two of those went out of business with the economic downturn. But it wasn't all bad during that time; in fact, most were home runs. For example, we bought one for $280,000 in Newport, RI, spent $15,000 per unit to upgrade, and then sold them off as condos for $155,000 each. We did many of these.

Finally, there were the buildings we kept as multifamily rentals. With no profit coming in from the other properties to fix up or even properly maintain those apartment buildings, we had no exit path from those purchases, as they were not attractive to buyers unless offered at less than what we owed or what bankers call a **short sale**. The banks forgave debt during the crash for some individual property owners but fought to collect from investors, although eventually they had to write off debt or settle on short sales with us.

SHORT SALE:

Any sale of real estate that generates profit less than the amount owed on the property.

At the time, we took a big hit. But since then, we've more than made up for losses by profiting on the many lessons learned from 2007–2008. And you too can learn from these lessons and avoid the same mistakes in your business.

Now that you know how I *used to* do business, forget about it—unless you want to experience the heart palpitations and the stress I endured in 2008. I have told you these details because it's important for you to understand that signing personally on loans, refinancing properties for cash-out, and not having a specific exit plan, as well as any deal whatsoever that does not create immediate and continuous cash flow, is *not* a good strategy. You can buy some properties and hold them, but I'll show you how to do so with both cash flow and a hedge against the market—without using your own cash or credit.

DIGGING OUT

I didn't survive alone. With the help of a supportive wife and some great mentors, I dug my business out of the hole over the ensuing five years. But it wasn't easy. I remember one friend, Cle Blair, a successful builder and business owner from Rutland, Massachusetts, telling me in 2008, "It could take you ten years. It could take you five. Whatever it's going to take, you communicate with people. You be open with them. You let them know what's going on. The whole nation is dealing with this. You be the one that speaks up and communicates well and remember, you didn't personally take down the national real estate market!" I never forgot that. That helped me a lot with dealing with the creditors, vendors, and investors, and I've reminded him a few times and thanked him.

Numerous attorneys and friends said, "You should just file bankruptcy. To heck with everyone." I didn't want to do that. We painfully went through setting up payment plans with creditors, vendors, and banks as necessary. The communications involved taught me many lessons we'll discuss throughout the book and that I use in coaching new investors and partners. (You'll see how I became passionate about helping others learn from my experience—the impetus for this book.)

At a certain point, I had to resume the focus on creating cash flow, which would be the real solution to satisfying the creditors, as well as getting ourselves back on our feet. I committed to spend half of each day moving on to new business. I set standards for that new business:

- no more personal signing for loans

- constant communication with mentors

- making sure that we bought only properties that could be obtained without using our own cash or credit

I call these standards buying and selling on YOUR TERMS.

As of this writing, we control 55–60 or more residential properties (pending cash-outs), mostly single-family homes. We either have title or control them through a **lease-purchase** or other agreement. But each month we are taking on new properties and cashing some out.

This book will explain in detail, with actual numbers, how buying and selling on YOUR TERMS works for the seller, the buyer, and us as a family business, and how we structure these deals on our own terms with the parameters of not using our own cash, not taking out a bank loan, and not risking our credit.

LEASE-PURCHASE AGREEMENT:

A contract in which a portion of the lease payment or rent is applied to the purchase price of the property.

Buying and selling on terms is the opposite of what I did from 2004–2008. I credit one of my initial mentors, Ron LeGrand, whom I met in 2005 at his $99 seminar that a friend invited me to. I was hesitant to go because my wife and I had been on a great run in real estate since 1991 and were not looking for something new. We had built more than 100 single-family homes, then bought a Realty Executives franchise for all of Central New England in 1994. Despite mentors telling me "you cannot sell a real estate brokerage business," we sold it to Coldwell Banker in 2000 for a quarter of a million dollars and then started coaching other real estate agents around the United States and Canada. Our team—consisting of one agent (me), one full-time assistant, and a runner for signs and miscellaneous personal errands—had been doing more than a hundred transactions per year and we had 15 affiliated agents averaging more than 20 transactions per year, five to ten times the national average. Having worked with real estate agents unhappily at first as a builder, I understood the standards we needed to establish to be successful.

COACHING YOU TO MAKE CASH NOW *AND* IMPROVE CASH FLOW

You may be wondering, *Do I have to be a licensed real estate agent to buy and sell property on terms?* I will go into this in more detail in chapter 3, but the short answer is that if you buy property under your name or your company name and then resell that property, you're acting on your own behalf, and you're not conducting a service for a fee, so *no license is required.*

I'm not a lawyer or a licensing expert, so you should consult a local attorney because state laws vary. You've got to be careful to have the proper paperwork and the proper structure to comply with state and local licensing guidelines.

Buying and selling on YOUR TERMS asks you to study and train to transact the kinds of deals described in this book. There's a lot of information you won't be able to absorb all at once. But beyond this book, we provide tools, such as **Joint-Venture (JV) Partnerships** and one-on-one consult-

JOINT-VENTURE PARTNERSHIP:
When two or more individuals form a partnership to carry out a particular project.

ing, for those interested in learning and applying what is introduced in this book.

Our JV programs help you immerse yourself in the learning that is one of three major factors for long-term success. The second factor is having the right tools, which our membership program provides— from live-deal videos, weekly-lesson videos, and live calls with buyers and sellers to the proper vendors and resources you'll need. The third factor is having us as a hands-on partner walking you through a successful deal from the lead generated to a check in your hand.

Our family business is based in New England but is expanding far further, because our ideas and the JV program are working across the country. We are helping our JV partners realize the same averages as our private family company for per-deal profits of $20,000 to $65,000—depending upon the type of transaction. Those profits aren't guarantees of course, and results can vary for myriad reasons, but readers of this book will learn how they're possible.

For example, we work with a man who has a full-time job as an engineer in Pennsylvania but wants to transition into real estate investing. Within 90 days we helped him into his first deal, which will gross him $66,111 over 24 months. On our website you can see how he describes, in his own words, spending years "playing around" with real estate by attending disappointing seminars and "failed attempts with some mentors." In a testimonial letter he sent—accompanying a copy of his first lease-purchase check after he started working with us—he said, "I jumped in not knowing what I was doing with some seller calls but I thought, 'What's the worst that's going to happen? They'll say no and hang up. . . . It was quite the contrary as many of the sellers were very pleasant to talk to and your scripts, videos, etc. on your website helped. . . . If someone would have told me that I could make over $66k on a $130K house, I would have told them they're crazy!"

His enthusiasm didn't wane and he sent a second testimonial letter when he made his second and third deals, in the same week: "I'm loving the $236,000 payday with you in three deals!"

Also in Pennsylvania there's Sean Hannigan, a police detective who understandably says he has grown tired of kicking down doors at night to bust drug dealers. He wants to be home with his family more. In his first 90 days he did a deal that will gross him more than $56,000 over three years. He recounts the details on our website and says, "Without Chris's coaching, the process would probably have seemed overwhelming, but in working with Chris, you learn to relate to people's needs and be system driven from a business perspective. It also helps that I'll pocket roughly $10,000 up-front,

Don Strickland, who made $66,000 and $129,000 in his first two deals as a JV Partner with Chris and team.

Sean Hannigan, police officer who made $65,000 deal in his first 90 days as a JV Partner with Chris and team.

$700 per month net income for 48 months, and another $20,000 or so when cashed out—I think that makes my coaching investment return approximately five times what I spent—not bad!"

Then there's Lilia in Virginia who lost money in the real estate downturn and was hesitant to reenter the market. Her first deal with us as a JV Partner produced a 24-month profit of at least $39,000 and the Three Paydays that we create on most deals.

To make that profit, Lilia called a homeowner who was trying to sell an empty home in Virginia while living in another state. You'll learn in this book how we find the most motivated sellers to work with, and this one was a good example. We structured a deal in which we would have to go out and find a cash buyer for this home within three months, and when that wasn't working out, I called the seller back and restructured the deal, which you'll learn how to do.

LILIA'S DEAL BREAKDOWN—
HER FIRST DEAL AS A NEW JV PARTNER!

PURCHASE TYPE: LEASE-PURCHASE WITH MONTHLY PRINCIPAL-ONLY PAYMENTS OF $503

TERM: 48 MONTHS

PURCHASE PRICE: $48,700

SOLD*: $69,900 WITH $8,000 DOWN AND $753/MONTH

PAYDAY #1: $8,000 + 1 MONTH RENT OF $753 = $8,753

PAYDAY #2: MONTHLY SPREAD OF $753 - $503 = $250
          X 48 MONTHS TOTALS $12,000

PAYDAY #3: $69,900 LESS $8,000 PAID = $61,900 DUE,
          LESS ($503 X 48 = $24,144)
          PREPAID = $37,756

TOTAL PAYDAYS: $58,509, IF FULL TERM.

*WE SOLD ON A 24-MONTH LEASE, AS BUYER WILL PAY CASH ON OR BEFORE THEN, WHICH WILL REDUCE PAYDAYS #2 AND #3, SO THE PROFIT MAY BE CLOSER TO $39,000.

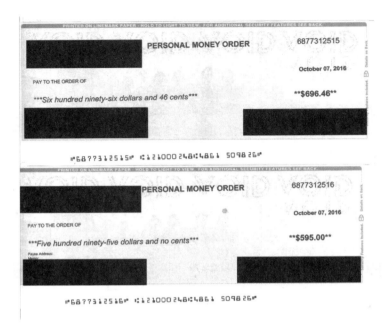

CASH FLOW ON YOUR TERMS

Is it worth your time to try buying and selling on YOUR TERMS? Well, you can decide after you learn in this book the value of the Three Paydays you receive:

1. The monthly cash flow per deal, averaging $409, or about $5,000 a year on terms[1] ranging from an average minimum two years to as much as ten years

2. The nonrefundable down payment up-front

3. The cash-out at the back end

When combined, the Three Paydays average upward of $65,000 per deal. I say *upward* because our paydays increase as we become more effective at managing deals and increasing profits. Is that type

---

1   Our averages at time of writing.

of money worth your time? Well, if you do a few of those deals per year it's more than most people make at a full-time job.

If you tend to be skeptical, take a closer look at the numbers in Lilia's first deal: It was a tiny home originally selling for $46,000, and a lease-purchase turned it into a deal with a potential profit of $58,509 over four years while the seller happily got more than the original price.

This book explains what we mean by YOUR TERMS and why buyers and sellers will want to work with you once you become a master **transaction engineer**, using the Nine Steps to Success that I will show you. We'll discuss the types of profitable deals you can make in real estate without risking your own money and how to do them in a simple, proven, and predictable way. You'll learn the systems necessary to generate the right leads in your area and how to convert them—simultaneously—to cash NOW, monthly cash flow, and wealth building.

TRANSACTION ENGINEER:

Someone who has mastered the Nine Steps to Success and is ready to do deals. A transaction engineer is able to look at a property-information sheet, debrief a seller, structure the right deal, and then place it in the right bucket.

Note to readers: For many readers of this book, making their own terms may involve learning some new terminology. So each real estate and banking term will be defined in a box alongside the text.

chapter 1

ON YOUR TERMS—
WHAT THAT MEANS

My son, Nick, was 13 years old when a snowboarding accident left him in a coma with doctors telling us he'd never walk, talk, or eat on his own again.

Nick, a good student with an outgoing personality and close with everyone in the family, was with his school ski club on Mount Wachusett in Princeton, Massachusetts, when the accident happened on February 5, 2003. I got a cell phone call in my car from the school—one no parent wants to receive. The woman on the other end said, "Your son has had an accident, and it is too windy to life flight him, so he's headed to the hospital in an ambulance." I headed to UMass Memorial Medical Center. As I drove reality hit me: *My son could be crippled or die.* If you have children and have never said that to yourself, you are lucky. My chest felt like it was caving in; my eyes welled up, which scared me even more, because I rarely cry. I frantically tried to leave messages for my wife to meet me at the hospital. When Kim arrived we didn't have words—we just embraced. Shortly after Kim arrived, the emergency room staff came out with a bag of Nick's clothes and boots, which had to be cut from his body.

We would learn later that it had been icy that day on the slopes. Nick, an accomplished athlete and experienced, aggressive snowboarder, went off a 25-foot jump and at the very top caught an edge with his snowboard. He had forgotten his helmet that day and when he hit the ground he tumbled, causing multiple brain injuries. He was spared more severe brain damage—or possible death—only because of the presence of one of only three or four paramedics in all of New England qualified to perform an intubation, the delicate procedure of putting a tube down his throat for oxygen to flow.

More than six hours after I received that first phone call, we finally were allowed to see Nick. No other moment in my life has been that shocking and intense. We entered a room lighted only by the more than ten machines hooked up to him. He was a shadow on the bed—a lump, not moving. I was scared and felt powerless. As the doctor explained every machine and what organ it supported, our minds swirled. He was in a coma. His head on one side was swollen like a basketball, and he had purple and black bruises all over his face and head.

Doctors came in to speak to us for the first of many consultations and decisions about Nick's life that would become a normal part of our day for the next 85 days. Our first decision: Because of the pressure in Nick's head, the surgeon needed permission to drill a burr hole in his skull for a catheter to relieve the pressure.

Doctors said to start planning weeks instead of days for our stay at the hospital.

As the weeks went by, each tube that came out, each machine that turned off, every monitor that switched off was a huge deal. A major milestone came when we wheeled Nick into Franciscan Hospital for Children, and his rehabilitation journey began. The second week there he was able to sit up with support from nurses for two minutes—another major accomplishment.

We started to fill the walls in Nick's room with affirmations. He still could not speak and had barely enough strength to communicate using hand signs, but he read the signs on his walls. Nick doesn't remember anything from the weeks he was in a coma but says his family's optimism and positive energy made a difference in his remarkable recovery. "One day I was in a wheelchair at Franciscan and I said to my mom, 'Am I going to ever be able to walk again?' and she said, 'Of course you are.' It's right then I realized that I would be okay," Nick recalled later.

He exhausted himself performing 12 hours a day of physical, occupational, and speech therapy. At night, when he was supposed to be resting, I would walk past his room and see him working with weights. Kim and I asked his doctors and therapists to all get together and meet with us to do game planning, something they had never done before for a patient.

"Nick was very much focused," recalled Kim Pinch, one of the physical therapists. "He was always joking, always cooperative—but he had a very specific task in mind." Nick made goals for himself: to be able to eat a grinder, drink a Coke, and finally jog out of the hospital. Nick did just that—and it was a lesson in setting clear goals and using clear steps, family support, and game plans to reach those goals.

Realizing that life events can happen at any time has informed my business decision making and inspired my desire to help others.

Thinking back about a time we accomplished the impossible by having the family work together as a team has been a lesson I could apply, and not just in the comeback from the 2008 debacle. Deals can go awry, as you will read in chapter 9. But just as my family came together for Nick, my family business comes together to help our clients by having clearly defined goals and the steps to reach them.

There were people who told Nick and us that he couldn't expect to walk again, people who didn't want to participate in the goal-setting meetings we asked for. But we set up our own terms and our plan to fulfill his goal of literally running out of the hospital. He also caught up with his class, graduated from high school on time, and became a real estate agent and motivational speaker.

Personal tragedy can hit at any time. Too many people think they can't find a way—as we did—to care for a sick child or elderly parent. They say, "I'm torn. I should be there, but I've got to run my business." It's awful. But if you set your business up properly on YOUR TERMS, it can and will run on its own.

This was the case when my father had a heart scare on Fourth of July weekend in 2015, and I left for Maine with a two-hour notice to spend some time with my brother and him there. It was also the case when Kim's dad had Alzheimer's before he passed away in the spring of 2016, and we made the drive to Massachusetts from Rhode Island probably three days a week. We wanted to, and we were able to do that. When my brother passed away in 2010 at the young age of 47, we were able to be with family each and every day we chose to.

As for Nick, after living in a ten-by-ten-foot hospital room for many months, he wanted to skip college and go into real estate after high school. I said, "Okay. If you're up for a strict curriculum, we'll put one together." With training from Ron LeGrand, Dan Kennedy, the late Zig Ziglar, and other mentors and friends, we structured courses, seminars, trips, and things that he could go to and learn. That became his hands-on curriculum for the next several years. He joined my investment business full-time in fall of 2014 after six years as a successful licensed real estate agent.

Today, Nick helps the buyers through the entire process from the phone call to sitting down and signing on their **rent-to-own** home or other terms.

THE TEAM BEHIND BUYING AND SELLING ON YOUR TERMS

RENT-TO-OWN:

A lease or rental contract that includes the option to purchase a home for a set price (with a down payment or deposit), monthly payments for a period of time, and then a payment of the balance of the purchase price. In this book, rent-to-own and lease-purchase are used synonymously.

Kim and I have a family business that focuses on helping people reach their goal of home ownership, which many thought they could never achieve. Our daughter, Kayla, is the general manager for our real estate and coaching companies and works very closely with our JV Partners, making sure they have proper forms, checklists, and whatever else is needed to successfully complete their deals. Her husband, Zach Beach, works on generating leads, acquiring properties, and training—working with our coaching clients and partners. He has been with us since December 2015. Nick has continually fine-tuned his area as a buyer specialist and has helped us almost double our per deal profits from down payments.

While we are helping coaching clients and partners with their income goals and real estate businesses, the family business also helps other buyers and sellers who, for various reasons, are in the real estate market. We get some buyers who are in financial trouble, while others have no financial challenges at all but still want to utilize our purchasing methods for various reasons; some of those include just time to save more of a down payment, time to show "seasoning" to the lender. On the seller side, we are dealing with people who perhaps can't get the price they need or want for their home. Maybe they owe as much or more than it's worth, and a short sale would damage their credit. Or they may be builders or rehabbers who want to avoid the expense of a real estate agent fee, or have accounting and tax reasons to not sell right away, but to get their maximum cash-out in a longer-term deal. We have many sellers who are retiring and don't need to sell but are tired of running properties they own.

On the buyer side, we have two main categories: People who have credit challenges and the self-employed. The credit challenges have always been there, but banks have raised requirements. The self-employed used to be able to walk into a bank and get a **stated income loan**. They have cash for a down payment, but their accountant may have helped them structure their business in a way that may have been tax smart but the bank now demands they report their income to the IRS differently for two years before they can get a mortgage. Their credit needs "seasoning"—but if they find us, they can get into a home in the meantime and lock in a price.

STATED INCOME LOAN:

The lender allows the borrower to apply for a mortgage based on income not verified with tax documents.

SIX BUCKETS:

The different options a seller can fall into:
1. *Assign Out (AO)*
2. *Sandwich lease*
3. *Owner financing*
4. *Subject To (ST)*
5. *Wholesale*
6. *Optioning*

In chapter 5, you will read about all the different ways we can structure a profitable deal while helping both the buyer and the seller. We describe **Six Buckets** that are different ways we can make a deal with sellers to take control of their property and get it sold. For almost every seller who calls us, one or another of the buckets is a good option. Making a smart choice of buckets requires data and experience, and that's where mentoring comes in. You can start with no experience if you are coachable, have the discipline, and invest the time.

A mentor also can teach you to recognize a true prospect versus a complete time-waster. For example, sellers who want over-retail value or want all the monthly income they can get out of their property with no willingness to share it with you don't really want to work out something on YOUR TERMS. We can save hours of time and a lot of headaches by using automation and systems to screen out people who really just want a conventional sale.

When I first started making these deals I hired a mentor who spent a good six months in the trenches with me. Each time I thought a deal was structured, I'd call immediately and say, "Is this right? Let me send you everything." Within 60 days we had our first deal done, but it was six or seven months before I felt like I had mastered the process enough to forgo that phone call.

In real estate we're always learning. We have to make adjustments in some deals. There can be expensive lessons if you're not careful, but you shorten the learning curve by leaning on somebody who's already done it. I've spent more than two hundred thousand dollars on training so you don't have to.

In chapter 3, you will see that there is a logical, systematic way to make deals on YOUR TERMS: the **Nine Steps to Success**. The first steps are essential for any business, but each one is quite a

NINE STEPS TO SUCCESS:

1. Locating seller prospects
2. Prequalifying seller prospects
3. Using follow-up properly and efficiently
4. Placing seller in the proper bucket
5. Structuring and presenting offers
6. Following up on offers
7. Signing or closing
8. Locating buyer prospects
9. Getting the property sold

learning step. We refer to someone who has mastered the Nine Steps to Success and is ready to do these deals as a transaction engineer. I think of an engineer as someone who figures problems out and comes to a logical win-win solution. A transaction engineer is able to look at a property-information sheet, debrief a seller, structure the right deal, and then place it in the right bucket.

The Mentors: Ron LeGrand of Jacksonville, Florida, has been my mentor since 2005. I met him at a $99 seminar. In the late 1980s he moved from being an auto mechanic to real estate. He has since done thousands of deals and teaches his techniques around the United States and overseas. I have learned so many lessons from him that I make a pointed effort to consult with him or attend one of his events at least twice a year. I am constantly seeking mentors and have hired a coach of some sort almost every year since 1995.

The Buyer Specialist: Nick Prefontaine grew up in the real estate industry, swinging a hammer and doing cleanups at condo conversions at age 16 and knocking on preforeclosure doors at 17, just a few years after his miraculous rehabilitation from multiple brain injuries. Franciscan Hospital for Children presented him with the prestigious Profile in Courage Award in 2005. Nick now specializes in working with lease-purchasers, while also helping our coaching clients and JV partners. He has spoken to rapt audiences at high schools, awards ceremonies, corporate regional conferences, business associations, medical center openings, and fundraising events.

The Manager: Kayla Beach is general manager of operations for Pre Property Solutions and Smart Real Estate Coach, handling over $15 million in sales yearly and the detailed organizational work behind the scenes. She graduated from the University of Rhode Island, where she was captain of the equestrian team and earned a degree in animal science and technology. She continues to enjoy riding and working with horses, while also working with and coaching clients and JV Partners.

The Acquisitionist and Coach: Zach Beach focuses on teaching in our Smart Real Estate Coach business, concerning how to generate leads and properly acquire properties. At Pre Property Solutions, he calls expired real estate listings looking for sellers whose problems we can solve and visits with sellers to get contracts signed. He majored in marketing and minored in finance at UMass Dartmouth, and he continues to sharpen his skills to educate others.

The Life Partner: My wife for more than 30 years (as of 2017), Kim Prefontaine, has worked with me in every capacity throughout my career. Kim and I met when we were 12 years old in middle school English class. She is an amazing judge of character. Her real estate specialty is construction projects, whether from the ground up or rehabbing, such as condo conversions or fixing and flipping houses. She is also an amazing interior designer. Her raise-the-roof projects, such as putting a second floor on a ranch home, earned a write-up in *The Boston Globe*. She continues to work with all of us, always bringing new and refreshing insights and ideas to the table.

chapter 2

YEAH, BUT (FILL IN YOUR SELF-IMPOSED ROADBLOCK HERE)

So you think doing a deal on YOUR TERMS is starting to sound great, but you don't understand how it works.

I'll start with a simple example. After forming my company, Prefontaine Properties, our first terms deal was in Middletown, Rhode Island. I did a direct-mail solicitation, known in the industry as a yellow letter because it appears to be handwritten on yellow paper. It arrives in an invitation-style envelope and is appealing and sparks curiosity, so it gets opened. This mailing went to people who owned a home outright with no mortgage. The owner of a three-bedroom ranch home responded. The value was $235,000, according to my **appraisal**, and the seller wanted a minimum of $220,000. Everything seemed fine there.

The seller agreed to a lease-purchase and wanted $1,500 a month. We were going to procure

APPRAISAL:

The process of putting a value on property, including land and buildings. Appraisals of real estate may happen for various reasons and arrive at different types of values. A bank writing a mortgage may place a market value on a property that differs from the eventual sale price because buyers are willing to pay more or less for that property.

the tenant-buyer and then **assign** the buyer back to the seller to handle. (This type of deal and other options will be explained later in the book.) The home had been on the market with a local real estate agent for ten months with no success, but in just 11 days, through our signs and our marketing, we procured a very strong tenant-buyer and sold him the property for $235,000. The buyer had been driving by the original "for sale" sign almost daily for those ten months but called us when he saw our sign because it specifically said "Lease/Purchase NO BANKS." The big difference there? *Terms.*

ASSIGN/ASSIGNMENT:

When ownership of a mortgage or other real estate asset is transferred from one company or individual to another, it is called an assignment. We have a legal equitable interest; first we procure the buyer, then we assign that buyer and related contract back to the seller.

We got a nonrefundable down payment of $23,500, which we split with the seller, and beat the seller's monthly target of $1,500 by getting the buyer to pay $1,680. Our half of the down payment, $11,750, satisfied us at the time as an adequate fee for assigning the rights to our buyer, although we have since learned that we can keep three-quarters or all of the down payment.

The seller netted $223,250—more than he expected—pocketed $1,680 a month for 24 months, and kept the title until getting the balance prior to the end of the term. The buyer had two years to fix his credit and get a mortgage to pay that balance. It was very successful for the seller and simple for us since the buyer became the seller's responsibility once we made the assignment. Getting half the down payment produced a nice paycheck for us, but you'll see that in the majority of our deals at Prefontaine Properties, we stay in and collect Three Paydays.

A more complex deal involved a two-unit property in Webster, Massachusetts. The source was something I did personally at the time—calling a FSBO (pronounced "fizz-bo," and meaning someone listing a home for sale by owner). The gentleman used to live in the home and was renting it out. He had the tenant from hell, who not only beat up his property but also stole his identity and ran up his credit cards. To say the least, this homeowner was fed up and didn't want anything more to do with the property. That is the kind of challenge that we can help solve and be paid well for doing so.

The mortgage balance was $169,000, and the property was worth $225,000. The seller, who was an accountant and particular with his numbers, agreed to a lease-purchase. We became the lease-purchaser of his property for the balance of his mortgage, meaning we would take over the monthly payments of $1,250. We wrote a term of 72 months to give the mortgage principal time to be paid down. We then found a tenant-buyer who would be able to get a mortgage but only after some **credit enhancement**. We sold the property for $225,000 with a $1,950 monthly payment to us, so we were clearing $700 monthly over the current mortgage payment. And we got a $15,000 nonrefundable down payment. The two-unit building suited a family that had the husband and wife living upstairs with their baby, and mom, dad, and grandmother living in the downstairs apartment. The area was not the greatest, but it was a fenced-in lot with an additional detached garage and a perfect fit for this family.

CREDIT ENHANCEMENT:

A process in which borrowers try to improve the reports that mortgage lenders receive about their credit-worthiness. Borrowers can repair blemishes on their credit reports by correcting errors and systematically repaying debts. It's very important to use the right companies to do this. We have used one for 4+ years with our buyers.

PURCHASE TYPE:
SANDWICH LEASE-PURCHASE

TERM: 72 MONTHS

PURCHASE PRICE: $169,000
(SELLER'S MORTGAGE BALANCE)

SOLD: $225,000 WITH $15,000 DOWN
AND $1,950/MONTH

PAYDAY #1: $15,000 NONREFUNDABLE DOWN PAYMENT

PAYDAY #2: MONTHLY SPREAD OF $1,950 - $1,250 =
$700 x 72 MONTHS TOTALS $50,400

PAYDAY #3: $225,000 LESS $15,000 DOWN LESS
$135,000 MORTGAGE BALANCE AFTER SIX YEARS OF
PRINCIPAL PAYMENTS = $75,000

TOTAL PAYDAYS: $140,400

This example shows the Three Paydays: (1) a deposit up-front, (2) a monthly spread, which is the difference between our buyers' payment in and our mortgage payment out, and (3) the back end/finance cash-out. Even after seeing how this type of deal has worked for us, our **coaching clients** sometimes doubt whether it will work for them. "Yeah, but . . ." they say; their market is different, sellers in their area are

COACHING CLIENTS:

Our website, SmartRealEstateCoach.com, has a members-only area, ranging from online video lessons to personal coaching, consulting, and Joint-Venture Partnership programs. See the website's Products pages for details of the levels of membership and current pricing.

different, or they have some other self-imposed roadblock keeping them from realizing their Three Paydays.

Let's go over those "Yeah, but . . ." concerns one at a time.

"Yeah, but," you ask, "didn't you risk your family's own money by taking on the mortgage?"

Actually, not much at all, because I only put down a $10 deposit and spent $125 on a title search when I signed my lease-purchase agreement, and our taking over the mortgage payment was contingent upon me finding my buyer first. Only then did we start making the mortgage payments. We always had a sure bet. The mortgage stayed in the seller's name until cashed out.

"Yeah, but," you say, " . . . sounds great . . . so why aren't more people doing this?"

Why wasn't I doing it during my first 20 or so years in real estate? Because this type of deal is not conventional. It's been done for decades, and yet sellers and buyers regularly say to me, "I've never heard of this. Is this new? Why aren't more people doing it? This sounds too good to be true." To take advantage of it, you only need to ask, "Why *not* me?" and come to believe that you actually can do it. And you have to learn how. The best way to learn is to grab on to the shirttail of someone (like me) who is doing it and allow him or her to teach you. Unfortunately, some of the few people teaching this type of deal just sell the idea without the deeper knowledge and experience that comes from actually doing deals. Regardless of what stage of my businesses I was at over the past 25-plus years, I always found people doing what I wanted to do and learned from them.

The learning curve is an important consideration. I ask people, "How old are you?" Let's say someone is 35 years old. My advice is, "Well, it took you 35 years to get here (and most aren't happy with 'here'), so be patient." If that person is a doctor, he or she will have spent a better part of nine years in college but may be making $150,000 or $200,000. If that person is a judge, he or she may have spent upward of eight years in college and many more years practicing law to be making $100,000. Whatever profession—teacher, architect, CPA—nothing else out there that I'm aware of, including franchises, can provide so much return for the time invested in learning and practicing as being a transaction engineer on YOUR TERMS. More on patience and timing will be found in chapter 10.

"Yeah, but," you ask, "don't you need special credentials or licensing?"

Having been a real estate agent and having owned a real estate brokerage, I understand there are different perspectives on this question, and it is very important to disclose one's credentials and role. Anyone can become a transaction engineer and do deals on YOUR TERMS if you are willing to take the time to develop the skill sets necessary (the transaction engineer's Nine Steps to Success will be detailed in the next chapter). You can't skip steps or think you can just push a button or buy a magic product and have instant success.

Generally speaking, if you have an equitable interest in a property or own a property, you are acting on your own behalf and are not conducting a service for others for a fee and, as such, you do not need a license.

Some states *do* require a license to assign an option. With the advice of a local attorney, you can adapt YOUR TERMS, or you can add a real estate agent to your team. In Florida, a person who is not a principal in the company needs a license. For example, if you hire an acquisitionist on your team—like Zach is for us—he or she needs a license.

I can tell you that my son Nick, and I both resigned our real estate licenses when we got into buying and selling on OUR TERMS. We also have JV Partners right now who are licensed. There are two sides to this question on licensing. For me, I just didn't want to deal with the drama of having real estate agents calling me to scream and whine that I was trying to "steal" their listing because their client received some of our marketing materials, which go out to general geographic areas. Since I am not a licensed real estate agent any longer, I don't get those calls. There's a disclosure on my website written by my attorney that says the following:

> *Prefontaine Properties and affiliated or subsidiary companies are not real estate brokers or agents. Prefontaine Properties is a real estate investment company. Prefontaine Properties is not a real estate brokerage and does not provide realtor services to the public, or to any of the parties to which it has contractual relationships.*

My website disclosure goes on to say that if you are selling a home, we can purchase it, any price, condition, or area. We also can pay cash and close in five days from clear title, or we can structure a lease-purchase with you. That is a legal disclosure that my attorneys wrote to be very clear to the public that we are not providing a service. We are purchasing property and/or controlling it and then offering it out to the public. Check with your attorney for appropriate disclosure guidelines for your area.

Also, if you're not going to go out and practice as a real estate agent, and you just want to be an investor, why waste a lot of hours and fees to keep up with barely relevant continuing education required to keep a real estate license? And if you are a real estate agent in a company owned by someone else, that broker-owner will rightfully be entitled to a piece of your deal profits.

Readers already licensed may not want to give up their real estate license if their goal is just to add income streams. For example, they could note on a listing, "We have terms. We have owner financing." There are very few such listings. A real estate agent who becomes known as the terms expert can help almost any buyer or seller and can get some commissions through referrals from real estate agents who don't have another solution for some of their buyers and sellers. On the flip side, a terms expert may be working with a seller who, for whatever reason, decides to do a conventional sale, and the investor who is a licensed agent can pick up that commission. Since even my mentors have differing opinions on this subject, you will need to decide for yourself.

Our approach is to refer conventional sellers to real estate agents, who can't legally pay us for that referral but do share comparative market-analysis information and refer business back to us. We no longer need a real estate agent to give us access to expired listings on the Multiple Listing Service, because anyone can see a flood of these now by using one of the available services we have on our website.

One other advantage of having a real estate license is that, as a service covered by your license, you can assign a lease-purchase back to the seller—like in the deal at the beginning of this chapter— without first doing your own lease-purchase contract. But clearly, I think the disadvantages of having a license outweigh the advantages.

"Yeah, but," you say, "I don't have the money to get started."

Remember, I started this when I was just coming back from the downturn and had little to no capital. I was restructuring my business and couldn't spend money hiring someone to call prospective sellers.

I went through expired home-sale listings and FSBO ads and made calls myself, using scripts. I started off very slowly with a few hours a few mornings a week. Only after the first deal described at the beginning of this chapter brought in an $11,750 down payment did I start to invest cash back into the business to ultimately grow it to where it is today, with our kids involved.

If you think about the average deal proceeds mentioned in this book's introduction—$409 monthly (for 24–48 months!), about $20,000 up-front, about $30,000 on the back end—just one of those deals is enough to fund an assistant to do calls and begin to very slowly, very carefully, very conservatively scale your business.

"Yeah, but," you say, "I can't believe it's possible to start with no money."

Of course you need to spend a few hundred dollars at the beginning or maybe a few thousand dollars spread over time. A virtual phone system, which provides small businesses with professional call-answering and forwarding, may cost $25 or $30 a month. If you can't design a website yourself, you may end up paying someone to do so, but we have a web designer who can build a done-for-you site just like ours.

You'll need training. Our website has free videos you can access right now. They won't make you an expert but will give you an idea of how deals are structured.

Our website, **SmartRealEstateCoach.com**, has more start-up resources. For less than $500 yearly, you get about 15 hours of video training from me—basically the entire business via our *Quantum Leap Systems* home-study video course, but without the personal support I provide in my higher-end partnership and coaching plans. And in our Products area online, we have done-for-you websites that allow you to utilize our buyer and seller videos and more.

"Yeah, but," you say, I've seen other websites with other expert coaches offering different approaches, and I don't know whom to believe."

I only can teach what we as a company are doing. Find a mentor who is not just teaching but doing deals—*currently*, because things change rapidly in the real estate market. Do some soul searching about exactly what you'd like to accomplish, then find someone who's done it. Also, some personalities obviously would fit you better than others. You will know that after watching two or three hours of their videos.

If you've seen any of my videos you've probably figured out there's no hype and I'm pretty blunt and to the point. If that's not your style, then I'm not the best mentor for you. You be the judge, because you can tell if you have a personality conflict with someone. I'm not so naïve as to think I'm the only one teaching these techniques, but I know we produce deals at Prefontaine Properties—that's my goal, and that should be yours.

Training should provide you a game plan of daily activities needed to support your goal. In our case, we know what our numbers are—the specific number of leads per week of prospective sellers needed to produce our bottom line of deals per month. We have a team now, including a **virtual assistant** who locates the phone numbers and dials FSBOs nine hours a week.

We know how we got to this level, starting in 2013, part time, collecting our first check in September 2013 and two months later, with a little profit, getting our first virtual assistant. In January 2014, Nick started helping with marketing, and buyers started calling and e-mailing frequently enough that we hired a virtual assistant to call and screen the inquiries so I would have to talk to only those who were really serious. By December 2014, Nick became a full-time buyer specialist. A month later, I hired my first part-time in-house assistant to handle paperwork. In 2016, my

VIRTUAL ASSISTANT:

An outside contractor—either an individual or a company—that works off-site. Assistants work a set number of hours per week, using their own equipment for telephone and electronic communications and are paid a flat fee with no worries about payroll and associated taxes and fees.

daughter, Kayla, and son-in-law, Zach, joined the team full time—Kayla as general manager and Zach as an acquisitionist. My book-keeper had preceded all this and has been with me eight years.

The reason I shared this detailed timeline is that we learned through experience how to scale up the staff and outsource only when we can clearly predict that the extra help is going to add to monthly profits by five to ten times what it costs. This is what we teach our members. One of my mentors recommended to me at a private mastermind group[2] meeting to hire a part-time assistant—which I did—the week I got back. You've got to remember to reinvest in yourself once you start doing deals, and you *will* start doing deals. Ron said the yearly cost of the additional team member would allow me to do more deals, and boy was he right—again.

"Yeah, but," you say, "real estate is volatile and I'm afraid to be in a field where income might be very unpredictable."

---

2   For a definition of mastermind groups, see page 112.

Income is actually extremely predictable. If you come to me and say, for example, that you want to earn $100,000, I can tell you how many deals per year you are likely to need in order to accomplish that. We've determined how many leads are needed to produce a deal and what the average payout is. Eventually you will have your own numbers, but until then we've got a good average based on our own business and our Joint-Venture Partners around the country. The average person can produce five to ten leads a week as a beginner. If we know you'll need 150 leads to produce the $100,000 income you want and divide that by a conservative estimate of five a week, it's going to take you 30 weeks. So we can predict what kind of income might come from working two, three, or five days a week. We provide this to our members in a Business Game Plan worksheet.

"Yeah, but," you say, "I need even more income."

We have people come to us who are making good money, as a chiropractor, engineer, or police officer, for example, and can only get into this business if they can make upward of $300,000. We use the same formula so they walk out with a Business Game Plan that tells them how many leads they'll need per week and how to get there. For example, we know the average cash up-front on these transactions is around $20,000, so six deals would provide $120,000, *not* including the other two paydays. And our experience shows that everyone in our program should be able to do six deals in the first 12 months, and often more, by generating 180 leads total. That's not going to take long: less than five months, because even starting part time, as little as five or ten hours a week, our new investors are doing ten leads per week. With the monthly cash flow producing an average of over $2,400 per month in income from six deals to support automation and outsourcing, we've seen plenty of people make the transition to doing term deals full time in their first year.

THREE PAYDAYS (AVERAGE PER DEAL)

#1	DOWN PAYMENT FROM BUYER	$20,000
#2	MONTHLY SPREAD BETWEEN PAYMENTS IN AND OUT	$409 X 24-48 MONTHS
#3	CASH-OUT AT END OF TERM	$30,000
	TOTAL $65,000	

"Yeah, but," you say, "My area might not have the same kind of seller or buyer prospects."

Your local market may be different, for example, if homes there are selling great in the conventional way. That doesn't mean you're out of business with doing deals the way we do. It means you're probably going to have to produce more leads than the average of 35 that we used. A slow market may provide more expired listings for you to contact. And in any market there are going to be people who experience life events—like a divorce, a death, job relocation, or retirement—that make them prospective sellers. There are also people who just refuse to pay a commission to a real estate agent. Residential buildings with two units tend to work great for our deals because families are consolidating these days. Our techniques work on larger multifamily housing too, and our member resources include a spreadsheet set up to do the math on whether such a deal will work or not. If multifamily housing is abundant where you live, you may want to expand what you consider your local market to capture more single-family homes to make your business more well-rounded.

We live in a seasonal tourist area of Rhode Island with a permanent population in our hometown of only 25,000. The three-town island, called Aquidneck Island, is not going to produce enough business for us to do four to six deals a month. We expanded into Massachusetts, and when the market there started getting hotter, improving the ability for sellers to sell on their own, we expanded to Connecticut, which was still in a bit of a slump. You just have to look around you for the trends you can take advantage of or capture. There are plenty of towns or communities going through their own economic cycles.

"Yeah, but," you say, "how can I possibly get all the necessary work done?"

We teach about delegating and outsourcing. Thankfully, we're in an age where work can be outsourced to part-time contractors who can work on their own equipment from their own location. You read above about how we scaled up our staff gradually when it was clear the additional workers would generate more than enough profits. So much of this does not have to be hands-on once it's set up properly.

"Yeah, but," you say, "I don't want to be a landlord."

Some people don't mind being a landlord and take on deals where they will have to run a multifamily building for some time before they can cash out. I will tell you that we work directly with lease-purchasers in single- and two-unit buildings typically. We avoid three-unit buildings—and when it's four families and up, we use a management company to keep the units rented and deal with the tenants. In that case, our goal over time is to improve the net operating-income numbers and sell it conventionally at a profit. What makes that possible is the way we buy the building without risking our own money or credit—on OUR TERMS.

In one case, we put down the equivalent of only one month's payment of $1,023. Another time, we were paid at the closing table to take over the property. You can do this by carefully timing your closing date to immediately after the tenant rents are due for the month. For example, we closed that property on June 2. Rents were due June 1, so the seller had to come to the closing table with all the June rents, yet our payment to him (seller financing) was not due until July 15, after another cycle of rents had been collected. A limited liability company (LLC) owned by my individual retirement account (IRA) made the purchase and netted tens of thousands of dollars tax-free due to the timing. See the Appendix (page 149) for a copy of the HUD Settlement Statement.

"Yeah, but," you say, "I can't believe someone would give me a home or a building with no money down."

Our virtual assistant was calling around talking to FSBOs. He found a retiring college professor who had a nice four-unit building with no mortgage. Running the building was a headache, and the owner needed money to pay for kids going to college. He was asking $259,900. I offered him the full price if he would take payments over 48 months before he would get a balloon payment of the remainder. We agreed on a monthly payment of $1,023. With 0 percent interest, the $259,900 principal was going down every single month for four years—for a total reduction of $49,104. So at the end of 48 months, I owed only $210,796. Our net cash flow every month was $735, what we cleared after paying the $1,023 and all the management fees, maintenance, heating, and other expenses. If you add the cash coming in every month, a little over $35,000 in four years, to the **principal paydown**, the profit from the transaction would be over $100,000 if the building were sold for $279,900, a modest apprecia-

PRINCIPAL PAYDOWN:

Paying in installments the outstanding balance of a mortgage that doesn't include interest or any other charges. My favorite buy strategy and market hedge.

tion after four years. We may extend that term and gain more appreciation. We could also just sell prior to balloon date time or even refinance if we wanted to— multiple options.

The seller wanted his hands off the building immediately. Winter was coming. It's a very interesting time to make deals around our market with the seasons changing. Seeing a clear path to paying for his kids' education four years out was preferable to waiting for a conventional sale in which he might have taken a hit on his price.

"Yeah, but," you say, "what if the sellers change their minds before closing on a lease-purchase?"

We record what's called a notice of option or memorandum on the seller's title at the registry of deeds. This notice of option clouds the title, meaning they can't close on a sale without having a fee to us show up on their closing statement and have us literally sign off on it in order to convey with clear title.

"Yeah, but," you say, "the real estate market has ups and downs and I'm not convinced it is a stable field to go into."

When buying on terms, like we do, you are in the driver's seat if the market changes. First, on all of the examples I've given there's drastic principal paydown every single month. In all the deals we do, there is no **personal guarantee of debt**. Your risk is the $10 or $100 you put up. In all the deals we do, it's possible to pick up the phone at the end of a term when the seller is due to be cashed out and say, "The market has taken a drastic turn. I'd like to get an extension of 12 months, 24 months, or 36 months with the seller and the buyer" or "let's adjust the price to reflect the market." Or you can assign the deal back to your seller. It's important that the paperwork on all the different types of deals, which we'll describe later in the book, and which we have in our online membership area, is designed around what I have just described. We've spent tens of thousands of dollars with our attorneys, and you can have access to all of that.

PERSONAL GUARANTEE OF DEBT:

When you sign for a home mortgage, the bank requires you to pledge your personal assets to guarantee against default. A complete NO-NO when buying on your terms.

• • •

We've covered a lot of the doubts that can become self-imposed road-blocks for those afraid to begin investing in real estate on their own terms. I was in a panic after I bought my first house this way, asking my mentor, "Now what do I do?" He assured me, "You will never be short of buyers." Sure enough, that first deal went through in 11 days. Imagine how that would be for you to know you can possibly have a check 5–20 days after securing a property.

Ever since we started, there might be two or three per year that don't get sold. Our contracts, "contingent upon us finding a buyer," provide for us to just say to the seller, "We weren't able to do it." There are no hard feelings. It's built into the contract. But it's very rare lately to not sell one of the homes, because enough people are having trouble getting a loan and/or saving for a down payment large enough to satisfy the banks.

We've lived through all the "Yeah, buts" and created checklists, forms, proper disclosures, and systems to handle them. We have videos online—what I call real-life lessons—for our members to see how to deal with the good, the bad, and the ugly. The next chapter outlines the business process and how you become a transaction engineer.

chapter 3

NINE STEPS TO BECOMING A MASTER TRANSACTION ENGINEER

"You may not remember me," said the caller. I did remember him, but more important, he remembered liking what he had heard during a meeting my son and I had with him and his brothers seven months earlier. They had been liquidating an estate after their father's death and had a house to sell, which they ended up doing by using a real estate agent. A conventional home sale happens often in probate, because at least one of the heirs inevitably is eager to get cash right away.

The caller said he and his wife owned "another home here we'd like you to buy with owner financing like you had suggested, and we've got to leave to go to South Carolina in four days, so we'd like to do this right away." Needless to say, Nick and I visited right away. The single-family home in Massachusetts had been listed with a real estate agent at around $200,000, but I estimated the value at $220,000. We ended up negotiating a purchase price of $183,900 with zero down. I will explain owner-financing deals in more detail in chapter 5, but basically the seller was going to play the role of the bank and take monthly principal payments of only $923 per month for 48 months, after which we would owe the remaining balance—but with no interest payments on the $183,900.

Our **exit** strategy as always was to find a rent-to-own buyer, which we did. The buyer agreed to pay $239,000 but would start by giving us a $15,000 down payment and paying us $1,500 a month in a 36-month lease, which provided a buffer on our 48 months to cash out with the seller. So again we were getting Three Paydays: $15,000 down was Payday #1.

EXIT:

In our transactions, exit refers to how we're going to sell a property we control.

The difference between our paying the seller $923 a month and collecting from the buyer at $1,500 is a spread of $577 a month, Payday #2. And since the $923 a month was all paying down principal, unlike a traditional mortgage in which only a tiny piece of the early payments would have gone to principal, the profit on this deal after four years is around $128,000, including Payday #3—the final difference between the selling price of $239,900 minus the down payment and what we owe at the end of the deal.

PURCHASE TYPE:
OWNER FINANCING

TERM: 48 MONTHS

PURCHASE PRICE: $183,900 INCLUDING MONTHLY PAYMENTS OF $923 PRINCIPAL-ONLY FOR 48 MONTHS, THEN A BALLOON PAYMENT OF THE BALANCE

SOLD: $239,900 WITH $15,000 DOWN AND $1,500/MONTH FOR 48 MONTHS

PAYDAY #1: $15,000 NONREFUNDABLE DOWN PAYMENT

PAYDAY #2: MONTHLY SPREAD OF $1,500 – $923 = $577 X 36 MONTHS TOTALS $20,772

PAYDAY #3: $239,900 LESS $15,000 DOWN, LESS $139,595 OWED TO SELLER AT END OF TERM (PURCHASE PRICE MINUS 48 X $923 PREPAYMENT OF $44,304 = $85,305

TOTAL PAYDAYS: $121,077

The homeowners got about the same price they would have gotten after paying a real estate commission in a conventional sale. With winter coming, and them wanting to retire to the Carolinas, they didn't care that they were getting their price over time in payments. They had done their homework on us seven months prior and felt they could trust us. And importantly, we were able to buy on five days' notice and pay the seller's closing costs—a couple of thousand dollars. In those five days, we protected ourselves by doing a **title search** on the property and having the attorney process paperwork that the seller would sign, including giving us the right to call off the purchase or renegotiate if the property had any liens or other unexpected problems.

TITLE SEARCH:

A public-records check to ensure that the seller is the legal owner of the property and that there are no liens or other claims outstanding.

This owner-financing deal may seem like a quick transaction, but it actually illustrates the methodical Nine Steps to Success we introduced in chapter 1.

All nine steps are critical to any business. In the real estate world, if you were to miss one step, you wouldn't have a deal because each step builds upon the other.

NINE STEPS TO SUCCESS

1. Locating seller prospects

2. Prequalifying seller prospects

3. Using follow-up properly and efficiently

4. Placing seller in the proper bucket

5. Structuring and presenting offers

6. Following up on offers

7. Signing or closing

8. Locating buyer prospects

9. Getting the property sold

1. LOCATING SELLER PROSPECTS

Any business is dead without lead generation, which for us means finding **seller prospects**. In the highly profitable Massachusetts home purchase at the beginning of this chapter, we were using expired real estate listings to generate leads and had located the seller more than seven months earlier when the family was selling a different house.

SELLER PROSPECTS:
Someone who is likely to sell their property and is actively looking for buyers. Not someone just throwing their home on the market to see if they can get top dollar.

But let's take a more general look at how a business generates leads, regardless of the specific type. It involves training yourself (and then others) to systematically and automatically generate leads from the right places but also being prepared to handle any lead that comes your way. And that involves getting the right information.

To be a transaction engineer, you have to find homes for sale, and the FSBOs are our top lead source. You can find them online, like everybody else can. And obviously you can find them by spotting "for sale by owner" yard signs. People say, "Well, if they have a sign they must also have an ad," but that's not true. Many sellers stick a sign in the yard as their sole means of marketing, which makes it one of the highest-quality leads you can get. We have a system that teaches you how to develop field agents looking for those signs. You literally have people driving around your market area looking for FSBO signs because they are valuable enough leads that you can compensate them well for the information. We have a detailed report in the membership area that outlines how to launch your own field-agent program. You or they can find signs by driving a different way to work or to appointments. It can also be done by letting yourself get lost in areas you wouldn't ordinarily drive through.

Real estate agents put the homes they are selling on a multiple listing service. Those that have not sold are referred to as expired listings. These homeowners can be strong seller prospects if they are frustrated by the failure of their real estate agent. Expired listings have been our second-biggest source of leads and may be the top source by the time you read this. We have outsourced calling these listings to assistants, but Zach and other team members are handling a lot of the calls, and I don't mind getting on the phone myself with "expireds" to stay on the cusp of the market. In fact, Zach has some new automation that allows him to get approximately 20-plus leads weekly just from expired listings.

Direct mail is another great lead source. We use the yellow letter, which is in a handwritten font on legal-looking paper delivered in a small envelope that looks like it could be a wedding or birthday-party invitation. The goal is to get the homeowner to open the letter. Many of my coaching clients have checked into alternative forms of direct mail such as postcards, but these do not get the same results, and that's been tested all over the country tens of thousands of times. For our few commercial-property mailings, we use a standard letterhead and business envelope.

The resource section of our website, SmartRealEstateCoach.com, has contact information for the company we use to generate these letters and for the list brokers that provide us homeowner addresses and phone numbers. Companies that specialize in real estate data are quick and easy to work with and can send a properly formatted mailing list directly to the company that produces and sends the yellow letter. Many other list brokers can be found by searching the Internet, but you need to decide the target of your mailing.

Because lists can be broken down by price range and factors such as number of bedrooms or whether the property has a garage, we can focus a mailing on what we determine is our sweet spot. This will vary by market. We tend to focus on the $190,000 to $590,000 price range. Higher-end properties bring nice paychecks, but those within a couple hundred thousand dollars in either direction from the market median sell faster. We also tend to focus on homes with three or more bedrooms. Your mailing budget and goals determine how much you want to narrow the list by categories.

Our online-resource section will point you to a company that provides a list of people who have inherited homes. These properties have good potential for terms deals because many are free and clear of mortgage debt or inherited by people who are motivated sellers because they don't want to pay an existing mortgage.

We also have had success with lists of homes with no equity, where the owner owes about what it's worth or even more, and homes owned debt free. Either way, we have deal structures that would work for those sellers. Generally, the debt-free homes have produced much larger Payday #3s, because 100 percent of the monthly payments to the seller go toward paying down the purchase price.

Last I'll mention a list that a lot of investors target—but we stay clear of: homes in or nearing foreclosure. Often these homeowners will tell you they don't want to sell, because at that point, they are focused on not losing their home to the bank. This is a list that can be worked effectively, but it's not my preference. If you decide to do so, you should consult a local attorney about complying with consumer-protection laws, which increasingly restrict making contact with those homeowners. Alternatively, let those sellers find *you* via your website or other marketing, and you can deal with them case by case.

Targeting any of these lists with yellow letters is just like any other marketing: You have to test it and then test it again until you get one absolutely cranking. If a mailing to a particular zip code or niche fails to produce a deal or minimum response rate, drop it. We help our coaching clients set that minimum based on our history. We know that a mailing of 1,800 to 3,000 pieces always results in our buying at least one home—not a bad investment for the cost of about $1.25 per letter. While we get most of our leads by calling prospects, direct mail fills in the lead flow during the holidays when phone response slows and in early spring when many people in our New England territory are selling conventionally.

A smaller source of lead generation is print and online advertising. Look for free classified ad sites in your market where you can run "I Buy Houses" ads. There are plenty of sites besides the well-known Craigslist. Calls from these ads are always trickling in, one to three a month, and you never know when one is going to be a hot lead. We recently got steady leads from an ad saying, "Local company looking to lease 3–4 homes in your area." I no longer run print ads, but they might be effective in a small or rural community.

We've recently been doing searches through real estate multiple listing services for phrases like "rent-to-own," "lease-purchase," or "owner financing," and that is bringing in leads as well. (Of course, it entails calling real estate agents, though this is made easier by following a script.)

The company that designed and maintains our website also makes sure we show up prominently in search engines (like Google) and social media (like Facebook). I can't quantify the results, but I believe that once you have cash flowing, it is worthwhile to spend some money on social media and **search-engine optimization**. The company that does all of this for us is listed in our online resources.

We don't rely on one type of lead source, because having a variety of seller prospects is more likely to provide a constant flow of leads. Following the cliché advice of "don't put all your eggs in one basket," we constantly update our online resources with the most current lead sources.

SEARCH-ENGINE OPTIMIZATION:

SEO is the process of editing your website or web pages in ways that help them rank high in the results of Internet searches performed by people you are trying to reach, whether or not you are paying for ads to show up in search results.

2. PREQUALIFYING SELLER PROSPECTS

When we began discussing how to locate seller prospects, I mentioned that it involves getting the right information. Whether you or your team are calling prospects, or they call in response to a yellow letter, following a script is the best way to screen for those who are serious and motivated to sell—the **prequalified prospects.**

One of my mentors constantly reminded us that asking

PREQUALIFIED PROSPECTS:

Motivated, prescreened individuals ready to do a deal on terms.

the right questions will help you determine a prospect's motivation and all the other information you need. Our property-information sheets have our scripts built in, and our team uses and continuously tweaks them as necessary. You can find those in our online-resource area. For example, depending on the situation, we might ask the following:

- "Is it by chance listed with a real estate agent right now?"

- "What is the asking price, and how did you arrive at it?"

- "Are there repairs and/or upgrades needed today that we should be aware of?"

- "If you were going to do any upgrades, what would you do?"

- "Why is it that you're selling?"

That last question comes nicely after the prospect tells you how great the home is. It's the most important question in revealing whether a prospect is saying "NO" or "no, not now" to a terms deal. Just listening and understanding why a prospect is selling is critical because that will tell you if there's a huge motivation or if that person is just fishing around a bit. "When do you want to be moved, ideally?" is a question that goes with motivation and will tell you where you need to move ahead next in the conversation.

If it's an expired listing, a good question is, "Did you get any feedback as to why it didn't sell?" Again, let the prospect talk. He or she will talk. Whether that person blames something on the real estate agent, the market, or the buyers, he or she will explain to you what has happened so that you can then see how aggressive (or not) you can get on your price.

Of course, before we spend time asking most of these questions, we make sure we are talking to serious sellers, not just any crazy callers. We direct calls generated by the yellow letters to a live virtual assistant for prescreening, since some people are just calling to say something like, "Why did you mail that letter to me? My house is not for sale" or "How did you know my house was for sale?" We've had some who suspected they were being scammed and called the police, who came to our office—and once to my home!—to investigate and then had a good laugh and moved on. Don't let that alarm you—the main reason is because the letters work best if they contain no business card or formal letterhead; a few out of several thousand recipients are questioning.

Our virtual assistant will weed out the complainers, the curious, and the crazy and send us only the ones who seriously want to talk with us. That screening is done on a simple property-information sheet like all the other leads that our virtual assistant sends us. An initial call to those people usually takes just minutes. It takes about an hour to call and talk with, or leave messages for, the 10 or 12 leads that a new investor typically gets in a week. Obviously there is then some follow-up needed from those calls and callbacks.

3. USING FOLLOW-UP PROPERLY AND EFFICIENTLY

Ideally the scripted questions on our property-information sheets—including "What do you owe? What are your monthly payments?"—lead to us asking them directly if they will be open to having us buy on terms. If they say yes to terms, either lease-purchase or owner financing, then we have a formatted e-mail that goes out with a full explanation of the terms, with the pros and cons. If they say no to terms, we move on to another prospect but still have a system to follow up properly and efficiently. Each month, many sellers call back as a result of our automated follow-up, techniques we make available to members and partners.

Deciphering which leads to spend time on is very important. The information sheet may say that a seller said no to terms, but what's more important are the answers that affect motivation: "Job relocating, six months; divorce, have to leave the state, two months; health reasons, have to leave the state, four months." Anything like that, we're going to very politely and professionally follow up and be there for them if they change their minds about selling on terms.

Homeowners who put up a yard sign or place a FSBO ad online honestly think they can sell their home themselves or they would not have tried. So, you have to give them some time. Usually if you call them early in the process, it is going to take some follow-up. Just understand that and don't be frustrated with that.

If we threw away all the prospects that said they were not selling they would not consider selling on terms, we would be throwing away hundreds of thousands of dollars. It's a truism in real estate that the money is in the follow-up. Life happens to people, and their circumstances change over time, which means their housing needs change. So we have scripts for follow-up calls to people who in an initial call rejected selling on terms. You can find these scripts and the e-mail explanation of the terms in our online resources.

As I was writing this book, I received a call from a homeowner I vaguely remembered. About a year earlier he had been contacted as a result of an expired listing, but he said he was trying for sale by owner. He and I had three calls. He seemed like he was not a highly motivated seller but might be coming back to me in the future. So he went into the file system, which meant he'd get a routine form letter later, the last step before a file goes into the wastebasket. From that letter, he contacted us, I visited the home, and three days later we put it under contract.

These blasts from the past happen a few times each month, and when you consider the possible profit per deal discussed earlier, it's very expensive to throw them away.

In coaching new investors, we have found that they are pretty systematic about returning messages and calling back those who already have expressed some interest. The follow-up most often not done properly is with the prospects who say no. So we provide a system to make sure that follow-up happens automatically and no one falls through the cracks. The system is not high tech. You can create fancy spreadsheets and use elaborate computerization if you want, but we simply put our prospects' property-information sheets into either a high-priority folder or a let-sit folder for follow-up and usually go through them weekly.

If we can't convert a prospect to an appointment within three calls, we schedule that person to get a final letter, and then one call back three months later. We don't call again after that. We call the three attempts in three months our 3/3 System. If we have an e-mail address, we send the letter that way and use a database system to keep prospects on our e-mail list until they opt out or reply that they've sold.

The goal isn't just to not waste lead—but also to not waste time. Even a new investor can accumulate at least ten leads per week, so there are soon hundreds of leads. Throwing them into files the way we do may seem archaic, but what we're doing works. Not all can be reached live by phone, so some get a message and an e-mail, which are scripted and available in our online resources. We even have automated dialers that leave a message with a push of a button and other systems that can leave hundreds of messages at a time.

By using our system when you have motivated sellers, you will know when to call them—or you will get a call back based on one of your form letters.

4. PLACING THE SELLER IN THE PROPER BUCKET

During the previous steps, we have been asking homeowners about their willingness to sell on terms. We have in our scripts (you will read more on these in the next chapter) explanations of the different categories of deals, or buckets, as we call them. We can engineer different types of transactions depending on how much equity or debt the seller has and whether the seller wants to keep or relinquish the title to the property.

To place a seller in the proper bucket simply means figuring out the best way to structure a deal. All deals are different, obviously, but they fall into categories. We particularly like those in which we exit by finding a rent-to-own buyer. But we begin structuring our offer based on the outcome the seller wants. Each one of our buckets will produce a different result for the seller and for us. And this is by far the biggest learning curve for transaction engineers. The beauty of Joint-Venture Partnering with us is we will be in the trenches with you actually doing these deals. There's no better way to learn how to navigate a deal and become a great transaction engineer than doing them with someone who has already done them!

5. STRUCTURING AND PRESENTING OFFERS

After determining what bucket you want to have the seller in, you must present an offer, attaching numbers to the structure of the deal. You can do that in person, on the phone, or by a combination of e-mail and in-person or phone communications. We help our partners lean on our company history in presenting the offer, so they have instant credibility.

We have found that some investors are wary of visiting the sellers' home, but building rapport and credibility in person is important, especially in a difficult real estate market and economic climate. Sometimes all the conversations with the seller to that point have been handled on the phone or by e-mail, and even if both sides are comfortable, we send a team member to the home whenever possible. Of course, an in-person visit can get a little bit uncomfortable on occasion because you don't know what you are going to find. We start by asking, "Is it okay if I take a look around?" And to keep it light, we say, "Do you have any animals, or do you have anyone that's not dressed?" Believe it or not, if we don't ask that question and sellers give us a go-ahead to walk through, we can run into surprises.

But going to the home has four advantages:

1. We want to view it and not just rely on pictures online.

2. The visit is an opportunity to go over all the questions and answers again because there will be nuances where answering in person will build credibility. A key nuance involves being clear about exactly when payments are starting, which is often contingent upon us finding our tenant-buyer. Some other issues that may have to be settled are whether inspections are needed for lead, asbestos, or mold, and if so, who is responsible. These questions are part of structuring the offer because they affect the deal's bottom line.

3. Sometimes the sellers may not disclose things properly or completely on the phone.

4. We can have the seller sign the offer on the spot, although I will explain why we don't always do that.

6. FOLLOW-UP ON OFFERS

Follow-up on the offer is very simple after going through the previous steps. That means we gathered the right information, the prospect was prequalified, and we presented the offer without ambiguity, either by e-mail or in person. The primary questions left to ask the seller are: "When are you planning on making this decision?" and/or "When is it best for me to follow up?" We don't want to be unsure of the sellers' timetable or what is convenient for them because then we can't follow up without risking bothering them.

Depending on the structure of the deal, we provide various documents and forms in our online membership area to complete the transactions. In most cases, the forms and paperwork have been customized by our attorneys after many hours and dollars invested by us.

7. SIGNING OR CLOSING

If we are taking control of a property by buying it subject to an existing mortgage, or with owner financing, then we are headed to a closing. If we are setting up a lease-purchase in which the seller is retaining the title then it's not a formal closing, but we still must sign a contract with the seller.

Depending on state law, there may be no legal requirement to have an attorney at a closing or even a notary public at a lease-purchase signing. However, for liability reasons and to make sure all parties understand the process, we have a notary on our lease-purchase signings and an attorney for all closings, which also need a notary. To become a transaction engineer, you don't have to reinvent all the documents you and your attorneys need. You can download the documents from our membership area and adapt them to your specific state. One of the documents for the buyers to sign, if they do not get their own attorney, says they were offered the opportunity to have legal representation and that our attorney represents us.

Another reason we don't usually ask people to sign documents on the spot when we go to their homes is the ease and effectiveness of electronic signatures. We use an online provider, DocuSign, which requires each signer to go through each page and check off with initials that they read and understood it, which provides us extra liability protection, in my opinion. If someone is physically whipping through documents, they could claim later, "Well, I didn't read that," or, "No one told me to read that," or, "I didn't know what I was reading."

8. LOCATING BUYER PROSPECTS

The easiest step by far, believe it or not, is finding a buyer for the property. Yet it's the step that haunts and scares new investors the most. They say, "Uh-oh, I tied up a property. Now what do I do? What if I don't get it sold? What if something goes wrong? What if I don't find that buyer?"

Chapter 6 of this book answers those questions, and we have a document in our membership area called "The Buyer Process" that walks new transaction engineers through dealing with buyers— starting with their initial response to an ad and following through to the actual signing. Having successfully handled hundreds of buyers, our son, Nick, wrote this document to assist all our members and partners.

When I first started buying and selling property on terms, as soon as I located a prospective buyer, I had to stop all my other activities. It's an exciting time when you know you have a buyer with a check, but there's work to be done: the initial meeting, handling the forms with the attorney, and getting questions answered. Now we can continue generating leads while working with buyers. It's nice when you scale the business and it's running smoothly with or without you.

9. GETTING THE PROPERTY SOLD

The time frame for speaking with a seller, putting the home under agreement, and getting it sold can be as little as a week or—on rare occasions—as long as 120 days. It is usually less than 90 days, and that's very fast compared with conventional real estate sales. (No whining and complaining from real estate agents here please! I know some of you can get it done quickly. I'm using averages.) If it goes past 60 days, we start looking at what the reason is. Usually it's the monthly payment. We can respond by lowering the rent-to-own price per month to the bare-bones monthly payment that we owe the seller. The idea is not to just break even but to bring in more buyer prospects.

As we meet with buyers, we help them work their monthly payment up if they don't have enough down payment, or we help them work the additional taxes due into the payment, preserving our Payday #2 cash flow. Ultimately, with the buyers getting in front of us and meeting in person, they are more comfortable working the deposit up with a plan—this is never something we try to push on the phone before meeting.

Another possibility is that we return to Step 4 and restructure the deal. That change can happen at the request of either the buyer or the seller. Remember, everything is negotiable.

For example, we had a deal (the bucket we call Assign Out, covered in chapter 5) in which we signed a lease-purchase so we could find a buyer who we would then assign back to the seller to deal with directly. As time ticked away, the seller found a new home and wanted to move out prior to us finding a buyer, so the motivation had changed. The seller, worried about making mortgage payments on the home being vacated, called to ask about another option we had mentioned in an earlier meeting, which involved us guaranteeing the monthly payment as of a set date. We said, "Well, we can guarantee you a set date to take over your payments whether we have a buyer or not, if we restructure the terms to a different price." We cut in half the $32,000 back-end cash they were owed, adding $16,000 to our Payday #3. We did this because we were confident we would fill the home with our buyer prior to having to cover the seller's next mortgage payment, or worst case, prior to making more than one or two monthly mortgage payments of about $1,600 each. We did fill the property with a buyer prior to the first payment and collected over $10,000 in our Payday #1! So we profited from accommodating the seller's needs.

Here's what the seller had to say:

I was trying to sell my house on my own with no luck for two years. Chris Prefontaine met with me and explained my options on the house. Chris laid everything out on paper for me with no hidden fees or questions. After reviewing everything, I signed up, and in two months Chris had a contract with a lease ready for me to sign. Signed via e-mail, and all is going smoothly. Very easy. Chris did it all. Very happy; got what I wanted for the house.

Narragansett, RI
$395,000
Mike & Melanie S.

See many more testimonials on PrePropertySolutions.com

The sale of the property completes our exit from the transaction, which we accomplish by systematically going through the Nine Steps to Success. The next chapter details what's involved in those first few steps.

WHAT ABOUT COMMERCIAL REAL ESTATE?

The deals described in this book mostly involve residential purchases, but the business model works for commercial properties as well.

While still in high school as a sophomore, our son, Nick, with money saved from washing cars in the neighborhood, invested with me in his first building—two commercial units that we rented out. Then when the building emptied in 2014 we said, "Why not do exactly what we do on all our homes—which is sell it on OUR TERMS?" We did exactly that, for a window-supply company owner whose goal was not using a bank. He has the master lease, runs the building, pays all the bills, and sends us a monthly check. He has a barbershop tenant in the other unit. We assigned our rights and associated lease for this barber over to our buyer, who put down $20,000 (Payday #1) nonrefundable and whose monthly payment to us is $200 higher than our mortgage payments (Payday #2), while our mortgage principal is being paid down over $700 per month.

We even had a property come to us once that had a commercial building *and* a home on it. The owners were elderly and didn't want to deal with it because the home was dilapidated. I said, "Well, I don't think it fits our business model, but what I will do is structure an option on your property for a price of $254,000. Then, as long as you're okay with it, I will bring it to market and see if I can get above that. I'll get the buyer, assign him or her back to you for an assignment-/option-release fee, and we'll move on." (This was done using a simple-option agreement, which can be found in our membership area.) The deal didn't end up happening that way. But eventually, along came a couple, Chad and Lilly, who wanted to fix up and live in the back house and start a barbecue ribs business in the front. We structured a rent-to-own, just like we do on a single-family home. We went back to the seller, who agreed to what turned out to be a very good deal. Unlike a conventional sale, it took a few years to get the cash-out, but he'd had no success with a conventional sale.

chapter 4

YOU CAN MAKE ALL THE DIFFERENCE

Working with the seller prospects you have located is really all about solving whatever challenges they are facing. It is a totally different mind-set from "selling" them on something. On the phone, your attitude is, *I'm here to fix their headache,* which could be debt relief, or changing the timing of the sales proceeds (on YOUR TERMS), or freeing them to move out of the area. But when a professional goes to help someone, as doctors, lawyers, and even lifeguards know, not everyone responds well. A master transaction engineer safeguards him- or herself against troublesome sellers by communicating properly and using proper legal agreements, or just by walking away.

I'm going to tell a couple of stories that may seem like bad scenarios, but they underscore the importance of never overpromising and being willing to walk away when you cannot structure a profitable deal that also solves the sellers' challenges.

One story involved a completely rehabbed home in Shrewsbury, Massachusetts. The builder who had fixed it up like new welcomed a lease-purchase in which the buyer would have 18 to 24 months to secure financing and, as such, would cash out the seller and us. We started sending buyers to look at the home right after signing our agreement, and the seller came back to us saying, "I really want six months." Well, that's not a realistic term for a lease-purchase because rent-to-own buyers need time for credit enhancement.

We understood the builder's headache. He had invested heavily in the rehab. Winter was approaching, which in Massachusetts and many other markets is a time when people start to panic about getting a home sold. But we had explained the lease-purchase process and the clear understanding was a term of 18 to 24 months—so when he suddenly wanted to switch it to six months, I said, "You know what? This is not going to work. We're going to get our buyers angry. We're going to get you frustrated." So, we walked away.

The other story is all too common and involved homeowners who came to us because they were behind on their mortgage payments—in this case more than three years behind. Since the bank had not foreclosed yet, they were basically living in the house for free. Based on what the house was worth and what they owed, they had no equity in the property, and so it was not worth us taking it on. Generally, we can't make a profitable terms deal with someone who is more than 12 months behind on mortgage payments—unless they have a lot of equity in the home. New investors still establishing their cash flow should avoid these deals.

Will there be difficult sellers sometimes even after you've signed agreements? Sure. That's reality, as you'll learn more about in chapter 9. The legal agreements we provide our members, which we've spent tens of thousands of dollars developing over the years, protect us from deadbeats and litigiousness. But even with that protection, we don't really want to deal with someone who is going to be a headache. There are so many leads in everyone's market that there is no need to deal with difficult people.

THE RIGHT SELLERS

Picture an old, historic tavern in a small city west of Boston that had been turned into a very large single-family home. It had been listed with real estate agents unsuccessfully at prices as high as $790,000. The most recent listing had expired and winter was coming, so the seller in Leominster, Massachusetts, was willing to sign a lease-purchase agreement depending upon what his price would be—have us find a buyer on OUR TERMS and stay in or assign that buyer back to him.

It took about four months, but we were able to find a buyer for $882,500, and get a $40,000 down payment of which we retained $22,500. That was our only payday because we had to assign the deal back to the seller, who began collecting $2,500 per month on the lease. Though we prefer deals with Three Paydays, this was a great example of solving the challenge of a seller who owed nothing on the home, was able to wait for our lease-purchase to cash out within 24 months, but just wanted to move out before the holidays, knowing the home was occupied through the winter. Someone else was paying about $1,500 in taxes, utilities, and insurance, and making sure the pipes didn't freeze.

August through November is a very busy time for us to take properties under contract because there is a perception among sellers that there are no buyers in wintertime. The market does slow down during the winter holidays, but there are always serious buyers out there for both conventional real estate sales and terms deals.

In our calls out to people with expired real estate listings, we got in touch with a couple in their late 70s. They were both real estate savvy and really understood the creativeness of terms buying. They had not only the property we called them about but also homes on the market in another state for about $475,000 and $675,000. Both homes were occupied by renters but had leases that were expiring. With winter coming and the prospect of having to find new tenants, the couple was interested in what we could do. We were able to find a tenant-buyer for each home within about 120 days. Because the couple was real estate savvy, they chose to have us assign the buyers back to them. We collected up-front fees of $20,000 and $36,000. They got the lease payments and were thrilled that both homes were then covering their expenses. Again, no Payday #2 and #3, but earning $56,000 from one expired listing call was not too shabby. How important do you think it is to understand and master our scripts? $56,000 important!

WHEN FSBO FIZZLES

A lot of times, when a real estate listing expires, the seller will *try* to take over handling the sale. I stress the word *try,* because 98 percent who try for sale by owner end up relisting with an agent or turning to someone like us to buy. Avoiding an agent fee sounds great in theory, and there are plenty of FSBO websites that encourage it. On the Zillow website, there's even a function that lets a seller set a Make Me Move® price. Some people get delusional and put a really crazy price in there, thinking it's just a number that they may or may not get. Potential buyers see the inflated price, see the house just sitting on the market for a while, and figure there must be a problem with it. The owners didn't know they were doing damage by throwing a high price out there, but the end result is an opportunity for a deal on YOUR TERMS.

Time is on our side in getting FSBO listings. Once the sellers have tried it for a while and gotten nowhere, they often respond to our follow-up messages. Remember from the earlier chapters—the money is in the follow up with FSBOs.

SINKING A BANK SHOT

Every week we run into homeowners who, sadly, have hit hard times—health problems, job loss, divorce, and so on. They try to talk with the bank and say, "We've run into trouble." All banks have what's called a loan-modification program where they'll restructure the terms of the mortgage, sometimes lowering the interest, sometimes forgiving some principal while putting it on the back end of a loan, meaning when they eventually sell. They're all viable options, but too many times I'm running into sellers who had a true hardship and the bank not only denied them a loan modification but dragged them out six, seven, eight, or nine months in the paperwork process just to say "No, we cannot help you restructure this loan."

By that time, they may be even worse off, especially if they stopped making payments in anticipation of a loan modification. That unmet need has created a huge pool of sellers we can offer solutions to. Banks also are forcing people out of their homes by doing this and then not foreclosing for many months, during which time the homes sit empty and in many cases go into disrepair. That's another set of opportunities for you as the investor to buy a home on YOUR TERMS.

Banks also have created two issues for buyers that have greatly contributed to our business. Since the 2008 debacle, banks have almost completely eliminated what they used to call stated-income loans, in which they wrote mortgages for people of means without the income verification of an IRS form W-2 or 1040 in the loan applicant's name. Self-employed people don't always report all, if any, of their income on the W-2 forms which employees receive each year from their companies. The buyers may have enough income, for example, but it's reported and taxed through one or more companies from which they draw cash that the bank won't recognize as documented income. Our rent-to-own programs give these buyers time to restructure how they report their income, which typically takes 24 months of "seasoning" before they can get a mortgage.

The second thing that has happened since 2008 is that banks have raised the bar on the down-payment percentage, credit scores, and other measures of credit-worthiness, such as **down-payment reserves**. These higher requirements have pushed a lot of buyers our way because our program gives them time to repair their credit and save more.

DOWN-PAYMENT RESERVES:

How much money the buyer will have in reserve after making the down payment. A bank might require a mortgage applicant to have a reserve to cover six months of loan payments and insurance premiums. Generally, the money has to be accessible and not in a retirement account. Banks look at the money's "sourcing"—it can't just show up in someone's account as a loan from a relative—and its "seasoning," meaning how long it has been in the account.

LIFE EVENTS, WITH OR WITHOUT STRESS

It should be clear from the stories in this chapter that some of our seller prospects had become financially overextended but others were hardly stressed out, even though all were dealing with developments in their lives that necessitated selling property. The owners of the Leominster home and the older couple with rental properties were very well-off financially and owed little to nothing on their homes. They just wanted to get a deal done and realize the best return financially. In this case, that was cash flow over time and best price—two outcomes not likely on the conventional market with a real estate agent or sale by owner.

Another example involves a building in my hometown that housed a tanning salon. A father and son owned the property. We contacted them because we saw a FSBO sign go up, and we then found out it was because the son had died recently. The father owned the building free and clear and was under no financial stress. But for financial-planning and tax reasons, it made sense for him to sell on terms rather than get paid all at once by a cash buyer or someone who would get an immediate loan.

Death, divorce, job loss, relocation, and other life events often figure into our leads that come to fruition. So, obviously when we see that kind of motivation written on the property-information sheet, there's more urgency for us to pursue the lead as they are seeking a solution as soon as possible.

COMMUNICATING WITH THE SELLER

No matter how perfect a match the prospect is to our way of doing business, neither you nor I will be able to consummate a deal if the seller doesn't understand the meaning and pros and cons of a terms deal.

In the last chapter we discussed our systematic follow-up that includes scripted calls and ready-to-go explanations that we e-mail to seller prospects. Learning to handle the sellers' reservations or commonly asked questions can be a challenge until you know the scripts, and that requires practice. When we first speak with many seller prospects about terms, their knee-jerk reaction can be negative or at least: "I don't want to lease my property," or, in the case of owner financing, "I don't want to get involved in being their bank." To that, we usually say, "Well, could you tell me what part of that you have a challenge with, just in case there's a misunderstanding?"

Almost always, the reluctant prospect has simply misunderstood what it means to do a lease-purchase or do terms. Sellers may mistakenly think they are becoming landlords, so the early stages of the conversation are geared toward making the possibilities clear: "If you got your full asking price—which you probably won't get on the open market—or got even more money, would you be open to hearing how we can get you there?" We explain we have different options, and most of the time they agree to hear us out. That's why the proper script and effective communication in the initial call are so important.

When we coach new investors or take on Joint-Venture Partners who are new at this, we emphasize the importance of studying and practicing the scripts almost like a daily workout. They also can listen in on our live calls to hear how the scripts play out with an actual seller, or they can listen to a recording later. And to take it to the next level, the partners will have me on the phone with them and their sellers at the outset so we are truly working the deal together. How many more deals do you think we could get working together versus doing them on your own if I or someone on my team is calling your sellers for you and with you? We have our entire team (family) to help you.

For example, my Joint-Venture Partner in Pennsylvania had a terms deal that had been agreed to in concept, but the seller had lots of questions that my partner was not prepared to answer. So he simply said he would call back with his senior partner on the phone, and together we made the call that resulted in structuring a deal on a beautiful ten-acre, debt-free property worth $500,000. Once again, the seller was under no financial stress, but just wanted to move on to his next property and make sure this one got handled properly. That phone call led to a six-figure, Three-Paydays deal.

STICKING TO THE SCRIPT

We know our sellers and buyers have 10 to 15 questions they commonly ask. So we have scripted answers that our partners can practice, master, and handle professionally. I can't think of any business that does not require (and benefit from) scripts for its customer communications. When you get a call from any telemarketer or visit a bank or store, they're scripted whether you pick up on it or not.

When you sign on with us for coaching or as a Joint-Venture Partner, the next step after you rehearse with the scripts is a training formula we call ACAA, which stands for:

Action: After you rehearse with the scripts, we want you to get on the phone and make your first three calls, which should be recorded.

Critique: Let's critique the recordings. Did you say the wrong thing? Did you have no energy on the call? Were you totally off script? Based on that critique, let's make some adjustments.

Adjust: Next time, why not stick to using our information sheet and prepared answers for those commonly asked questions? Let's fine tune how you handle your next set of calls, which brings us back to...

Action: Get right back into it and make some more calls, which we can also critique and adjust.

I used this process in real estate long before I got into making terms deals. People who do this continuously become more efficient and effective. A good example is my son-in-law, Zach, because he had no real estate background when he started with us, just a year ago at the time of this writing. The first two months of calls, he was stumbling through just like new investors I coach often do. Maybe the sellers didn't know, but I knew while listening for my critiques when Zach or our new investors were looking at their notes or fumbling for scripts. When I heard their first calls I would cringe. Five calls later, each one was like a new person on the phone as far as being scripted and superconfident.

After the calls became part of Zach's daily morning routine, he would send over recordings that could have been me or one of our experienced JV Partners talking. The practice showed up and there was more of a natural flow to the conversations. My son, Nick, also started by practicing every single morning. He would literally chant the scripts. Once you've done it enough times, repeating the same thing over and over again, you will get better and be very well scripted. To this day, Nick follows a scripted format as our buyers' specialist to make sure we are operating at the highest level.

A good way to practice is reading the scripts as fast as you can over and over again, not worrying about intonation, but just making the words become ingrained. By practicing answers to all of the commonly asked questions, you are ready for one when you get it. Some sellers only ask one or two questions, so it can take a while to get experience answering all of the questions you need to be ready for. If you can role play with someone on a regular basis, that's even more effective than chanting and practicing on your own.

If you don't have a mentor, or someone like me, to critique your recordings, you still should tape the calls and at least play them for yourself to critique. If you are thinking, *Man, I don't have any energy, I don't sound like I know what I'm doing,* then you know what you've got to do. You've got to go back and practice. It's an eye-opener— or, rather, an ear-opener—to hear yourself. And then (this is not an easy exercise), go ahead and play the recordings for someone who supports your goals and wants to see you succeed.

The Power of One Daily Discipline Chart

For many years, I have used this Power of One self-accountability technique to get done what I know I want to accomplish for the year. If I need to master scripts, for example, I break down the goal into monthly, weekly, and then daily chunks. The Power of One is to put one daily discipline on a chart, "Practice scripts 15 minutes," and make myself check it off the chart each day for the week or month it takes. The inspiration came from a mastermind group in 1996. A participant named Mike said, "You know, achieving our yearly goals is really quite easy if we simply break the goal down to a daily goal and then do what's necessary daily. This will allow us to win each day, and by winning each day, we win the year."

GIVING SUCCESS AN ASSIST

No matter how extremely well-scripted you are, the person at the other end of the phone may have zero desire to listen to terms or no motivation to enter our kind of deal. If you don't recognize this, you're wasting your time and you're going to be frustrated thinking you did something wrong. That's why we use the property-information sheets to assess who has the motivation to talk to us. We hit our targets by being systematic, not by changing the script each time a call goes nowhere.

As noted earlier, once we had the cash flow to pay for it, we began using virtual assistants to generate leads, so we would be talking to real prospects and have some advance knowledge of their properties and motivation. The assistants can work from anywhere in the world but must be fluent in English and any other language widely used in your area. I have coached clients who said they had no success with virtual assistants, and we found the reasons were the language-barrier and time-zone differences that occurred because their assistants were in the Philippines, for example. Assistants should be calling sellers during the hours you specify, when you believe they will find the maximum number of people at home. We have been sharing our trained personal assistants with partners for a cost that we calculate should produce a minimum of one deal a month for a small weekly fee.

I struggled with three virtual assistants before finding one I now have been using for more than three years. So, I can help with advice on how to find and deal with these remote workers to make them most efficient. You can hire the same people we use or find your own, and with the proper training, they will become an integral part of your team.

WHAT A GOOD LEAD LOOKS LIKE

A lead recently came in to our website for a property in Connecticut. It was a referral from someone else we helped in that state. I called the homeowner, who said, "It's been on the market with an agent, Chris. It's about to expire. I've been paying my mortgage. I love my homebut I have to leave for a job in Syracuse, New York. So, I can tell you, Chris, that I cannot make another payment." She said she had no equity in the home but was not going to walk away from it, because she wanted to protect her credit.

So I had a motivated seller who had debt and no equity in the home, which ruled out owner financing but meant I could set up a lease-purchase and fill the home with a tenant-buyer immediately. Even if her real estate agent suddenly came up with a buyer on the open market, she would have to pay the commission and closing costs out of pocket. I could solve her challenge by providing a solution with immediate mortgage relief and no out-of-pocket cash. This deal was done without us ever meeting in person and with a quick visit to the home by one of our team members. We put it under agreement with a buyer from our list that very same weekend—with $26,000 down (Payday#1) over time, $410 monthly spread (Payday #2), and a back end (Payday #3) of over $41,000. One referral, one call, one nice property. A deal checklist in our online membership area includes reminders to get testimonials and referrals, the importance of which cannot be overstated.

• • •

To the right seller, I can make all the difference, and so can you. The next chapter goes into detail about the six buckets a seller might fall into and when each makes sense.

chapter 5

THE PATH TO PROFITS: KNOWING WHAT DEAL TYPE TO USE

One of our Joint-Venture Partners in Pennsylvania put a beautiful property under contract, with the intention of it selling with **owner financing**. That is one of the six buckets that we put sellers into, and as I mentioned in chapter 3, it basically means the seller plays the role of the bank. But there's a catch in Pennsylvania for us getting involved in that type of deal because for us as buyers to purchase the property, we pay a 1 percent transfer tax, and we get taxed by the state again with a 1 percent tax when we sell. But we could get the same result for the seller by using a different bucket that we call the **sandwich lease**, and there would be no transfer tax up-front, because when we start the process, it's a lease, not a sale. We moved the seller from one bucket to another. The seller didn't mind, and it saved us more than $4,000 in transfer taxes.

You've already read a bit about a few of the buckets, but

OWNER FINANCING:

When a property buyer finances a purchase directly through the person selling it.

SANDWICH LEASE:

A lease in which someone rents property from the owner and then leases it out to another tenant.

I'm going to define each one and explain the pros and cons for the seller, the buyer, and the transaction engineer. In each category, we have spent thousands of dollars and hundreds of hours creating paperwork with the necessary protections for the investor. The forms are available to our members online.

ASSIGN OUT (AO)

Assign Out means that as investors, we're going to contract with the sellers to control their property through a lease-purchase agreement and then, once we procure the buyer with our right to do so, we're going to assign that entire package back to the seller to deal directly with our buyer. We then collect an assignment fee, or Payday #1, at the signing table with the attorney and buyer.

The sellers in this bucket retain ownership of their property because they're only doing a lease-purchase with us. So until the buyer cashes them out eventually, the sellers may see benefits in accounting for depreciation and getting tax deductions for interest and property taxes and more. The sellers also keep any spread between what they pay out in a mortgage and what we were able to obtain from the buyer in monthly rent-to-own payments—so they get that Payday #2, not us. For example, if the sellers' mortgage payment was $1,500 and we got a lease-purchaser at $1,600, the sellers would keep that extra spread of $100 a month. The sellers get most of the upside in this type of deal because we're stepping aside, not staying in the middle and collecting any of the profits. So the AO deal is not our favorite strategy. Why take only Payday #1 when you can have Three Paydays?

Sellers with a mortgage can protect their credit by being assured that their payments are covered every month by the incoming lease payments. Some homes are overleveraged, or worth less than what's owed to the bank. That situation threatens a homeowner's credit if they need to sell. A sale for less money than is owed to the bank is called a short sale and creates a credit ding. This AO deal allows time for the homeowner to pay down principal on the mortgage each month, using money from the tenant-buyer's monthly lease payment.

Sellers who are not in that bind also benefit from an AO because they get an income stream with no real net cost. As in the deal in the last chapter involving a historic tavern, they just have to wait for a cash-out, rather than getting it all at once as they would in a conventional home sale.

If something goes wrong during the process—for example, a divorce or job loss on the buyer side—the sellers are now dealing with that directly. They can call back the transaction engineer to fill the home again, but in the meantime they might be making a payment or two, so that's the big potential downside for the seller in an AO. Or they can revert to selling the home conventionally. They may choose to do that if the market has increased since they started, which could lead to a good outcome.

There are four advantages for a rent-to-own buyer in this *or any of our buckets*:

1. A very quick approval process, as in 24 to 48 hours. There is no bank or loan committee to satisfy—just us, the investor who approves the deal. We use a service, which we recommend to our partners, for prescreening buyers who need credit repair, as explained in the next chapter.

2. Immediate occupancy if the property is empty. And even if it's not empty, occupancy usually comes within 30 days,

unlike a buyer going to purchase a home and waiting 45–60 days, or sometimes longer. We've installed buyers into homes in as few as three days—a day for a buyers' meeting and a day or two to arrange and complete the signing with the attorney.

3. No real obligation to buy the property. The tenant-buyer has set out to buy the home and has put up a nonrefundable down payment but technically has only an option to buy the property at some point within the term. Buyers who get a job relocation, win the lottery, or have some other big change that prevents them from going ahead can walk away and not be sued.

4. A big advantage is locking in the home price. Renters trying to save money and fix their credit can get priced out of an upward-trending market. In other words, home prices could rise faster than they could possibly save. In a rent-to-own, once buyers sign the deal, the price is locked, and just like a homeowner, they capture all the upside appreciation of a rising market.

For the investor just starting out, an AO deal is a good way to generate cash flow quickly, with little risk, in a simple transaction. We gave an example earlier in the book of the very first deal we ever did—that took 11 days and had a nice profit of over $11,000. The transaction engineer puts up no money and faces no credit risk. The deal is easy to explain to a seller; as our members learn in the scripts, it is just saying, "Let me take your home to my market and my buyers' list and see what I can do." The transaction engineer is not signing on to make home repairs or mortgage payments but simply to find a rent-to-own buyer and assign back. There are no closing costs, although we always do spend a little money doing a title search. Morally and ethically, even though it is the seller's responsibility once we assign the buyer, we don't want to place a buyer in the home if there are liens on the property, not disclosed by the seller, which could cause a problem later. In only one of our hundreds of deals, there was an old lien the seller had forgotten about, and he paid it off when it showed up in our title search. He thanked us because the lien was accumulating interest as long as it went unpaid.

Several types of homes might be a good fit for the AO bucket:

- a home free and clear of any debt where the sellers don't mind getting paid monthly for a while but are just not willing to give up any spread or any back end

- a home where the mortgage payments are current but the sellers, again, are unwilling to share the sale profit with a transaction engineer

- a home with no equity, so no inherent reason for the transaction engineer to stay in the deal, but the buyer is willing to pay a sufficient premium to cover an assignment fee . . . as part of the price

- a higher-end home where the seller wants top price, and the transaction engineer is not comfortable taking on a high mortgage payment (or payment to the seller if no mortgage) and collecting from a buyer at that price level . . . if anything ever happened to the buyer and the transaction engineer had to cover a payment or two—ouch!

- a home whose seller wants the shortest-possible term

You'll see that in the other buckets when we guarantee a cash-out period, we build in a buffer of time in case something goes wrong. If we have contracted with our seller to have a cash-out in 36 months, for example, we may be comfortable accepting a buyer with a projected 24-month cash-out. With the Assign Out, we're finding a buyer and assigning it back to the seller right away and retaining only an assignment fee.

SANDWICH LEASE (SW)

In a sandwich lease, we're taking control of a property with a lease-purchase arrangement that gives us the right to sell the property, and we prefer to do so with our buyer in a rent-to-own. But instead of assigning the buyer back to the seller, we're staying in the middle of the deal. That's why we call it a sandwich. We're going to collect from the buyer, and then turn around and pay the seller or, almost always, pay the seller's mortgage directly to the bank. The lease agreement sets a definitive date by which we guarantee our buyer is cashing out that property.

As of the time of this writing, Texas is the only state I'm aware of that does not allow a sandwich lease. There are other ways to operate in Texas, which we will discuss shortly. In fact, as of this writing we have several JV Partners in Texas.

A sandwich lease offers an investor the possibility of Three Paydays. But if you are getting involved in such a deal, we advise you to have a protection in your lease agreement that allows you to decide when you start making payments to the seller or the seller's mortgage. If it is a large payment that would keep you up at night, you should start contingent on finding your buyer first. If it is small enough, or you've done several deals in the market and you know you can sell the home quickly, or you already have a buyer who wants it, you could just specify a start date. Many of our properties are sold within a week or less because we have a waiting list of buyers.

PURCHASE TYPE:
SANDWICH LEASE

TERM: 36 MONTHS

PURCHASE PRICE: $324,500 MORTGAGES PLUS
$44,000 CASH AT CLOSING

MONTHLY MORTGAGES: $1765.55

SOLD: $434,900 AND $2,100 FOR 36 MONTHS

PAYDAY #1: $35,000

PAYDAY #2: $334.45 × 36 = $12,040.20

PAYDAY #3: $434,900 LESS $44,000 OWED TO SELLER
LESS MORTGAGE BALANCE AFTER PRINCIPLE
PAY DOWN OF $296,500 = $94,400

TOTAL PAYDAYS: $141,440

Some properties that typically fit the SW bucket:

- homes that have no mortgage and a seller who is open to giving the transaction engineer good terms but doesn't want to relinquish the deed yet and doesn't need the cash right away

- homes where the seller is up to a few months behind on mortgage payments and has little equity (It may be worth breaking the rule about you bringing no money to the table if catching up the mortgage arrears for the seller leads to enough cash out at the end in the Payday #3. Catching up arrears is better done using the buyer's down payment.)

- homes where the seller has no equity but the mortgage payment is so low that the buyer's monthly payment provides a spread of several hundred dollars for you to pocket monthly (These add up. As of this writing our monthly total spread—all our Payday #s—is over $18,000.)

- homes where the seller is current on the mortgage but doesn't want the responsibility anymore, and the home is move-in ready and has a nice low payment

We had a deal involving a family with a home sitting empty in Rhode Island, as they had moved to Massachusetts and had lost their renter. Winter was coming, and several months had passed in which a real estate agent had failed to sell the home. The agent felt bad because the husband was in Baghdad, Iraq, serving his country as a civilian contractor, and the agent thoughtfully called us to see if we could help. The husband reviewed alternatives we presented and went with us, lease-purchasing the home, procuring a buyer, and assigning that buyer back to the couple to deal with. But I had some concerns about how that AO deal was going to work while the husband's job was keeping him in Baghdad most of the year. The wife, living on her own, would have to deal with any problem that arose with the home.

I explained that the sandwich lease would mean Three Paydays for us and a little less money for them, but they would be 100 percent hands off the lease-purchase and related buyer cash-out concerns. They agreed to be moved to the SW bucket so they didn't have to worry mentally or financially about the lease-purchase, which we guarantee.

Another example that shows the possible advantages of the SW bucket to the seller involves an elderly gentleman. I had made an offer to him to sell us his home on owner financing, which we're going to talk about next. He said, "I really love what you guys are doing. I studied up on you guys. I researched you online. I used to be in finance in the car business, so I get what you're doing. I want to do this, but I've got to run it by my attorney." His attorney talked with us and advised him that it was much safer if he lease-optioned us the property for the same price, with the same monthly payments—but retained the deed. So we structured a sandwich lease and placed a buyer in the home. We agreed to pay him $1,200 a month that would go 100 percent toward principal, meaning it was reducing our cash-out and maximizing our Payday #3.

In Texas, if you take control of a property by lease-purchase, and find a buyer, you can assign it back to the seller. Or you can control the property via a "subject-to" purchase and then lease it to the rent-to-own buyer. In that case, you actually purchase the property, **subject to** the existing mortgage, and then sell it to your buyer on owner financing or just rent-to-own. You just can't stay in the middle of a sandwich lease-purchase under Texas law. You can also buy with owner financing and then sell rent-to-own. You just cannot do a lease on each side of the deal.

SUBJECT TO:

A seller transfers the deed to the property subject to the existing debt staying in place and remaining in sellers' name.

Sellers may gain several benefits from a sandwich lease. If they are trying to qualify for another mortgage for a purchase elsewhere, having a lease-purchase, not a rental or an empty home, helps maintain their credit. A sandwich lease avoids the **due-on-sale clause** contained in all mortgages, so the sellers still have a mortgage sitting on their credit. Whether a bank will qualify them for another purchase obviously would be determined by their credit history, income, and other personal information, as well as the bank's policies—but at least they have an agreement with a definite cash-out on their current mortgage along with monthly payments being covered.

DUE-ON-SALE CLAUSE:

The terms of the mortgage forbid transfer of the property without fully paying off the mortgage.

Sellers in a sandwich lease retain the tax advantages of home ownership until cashed out. This means they will depreciate their property while still on the deed. From an accounting standpoint you are simply recording lease income in and lease payment out as an expense (whether it's a mortgage or a direct payment to the seller). The seller with a mortgage gets debt relief with a lease-purchaser taking over paying the mortgage. And depending on the structure of the deal, the investor may pay closing costs that a seller normally incurs in a conventional sale.

The sandwich-lease bucket generally provides investors the Three Paydays—cash from the down payment, monthly cash flow, and the profit at the end. We like this bucket for most of our deals. When it's time for a formal closing, your buyer would be closing directly with your seller and on the closing statement your company or land trust would be listed on the closing statement as an option-release fee or whatever the underwriter (lender) decides to list it as. This is because you would have recorded a notice of option or memorandum of real estate, so you are protected. One of the reasons this is so important is that the seller will now see how much you're making and could possibly get a bit greedy and want some of that—especially if your deal was originally that they get nothing or little out of the deal. The other issue with a sandwich-lease closing at the end is that you will have to track down the sellers and have them sign the deed to get this closing done.

OWNER FINANCING (OF)

For you as an investor, owner financing means you buy the property and the seller plays the role of the bank, carrying back a mortgage on any balance due. This arrangement works well for free-and-clear properties in which the seller doesn't want to get paid all at once. The big difference between sandwich lease and owner financing is that this deal involves the transfer of the deed from seller to investor at a closing.

All of the owner financing we've done has been structured with **principal-only** monthly payments. As the months tick away, our exposure lessens, so even in a market downturn, these deals are phenomenal. We can fill the home with a rent-to-own buyer, but because we own the home, we also have the option of selling it with owner financing to a buyer. We stick with rent-to-own buyers because if they default, the result is an eviction. If buyers default after you sell them property with owner financing, you have to legally foreclose, which is much more expensive than an eviction in most states that I'm aware of.

PRINCIPAL-ONLY:

Principal is the amount borrowed in a loan. Banks structure home mortgages so that most of the monthly payments in the early years cover interest charges, and the loan recipient only gradually begins paying off the principal. An owner-financing deal can allow for all payments to be 100 percent principal.

Sellers typically get a premium price for owner financing while delaying or spreading out any capital gains. By taking principal-only payments, they don't have to report any interest income, which is taxable. Currently, as I write this book, interest rates are so low that interest doesn't make much difference in these deals. We also pay the typical closing costs associated with a seller because we're not offering down payments and we cannot expect them to pay out-of-pocket to sell us a home that is debt free.

Since you own the home as the investor in an OF deal, you pay for insurance on the house, unlike the AO or SW deals, where the seller has to maintain insurance. That sounds like a drawback, but it actually lowers costs in the deal. We share access with our members to an investor-friendly carrier that provides much better rates than an individual homeowner would pay to insure a nonowner-occupied house. In a lease-purchase, the seller switches from a homeowner's policy to a landlord policy and requires the tenant-buyer to maintain renter's insurance for belongings inside the home. If the investor controls the deed, that's who must maintain landlord insurance.

Typically, the OF deals have a balloon payment due to the seller at the end of a term—for us often 48 months. The legal forms we use allow for that term to be renegotiated if necessary or desirable. For example, if you have a rent-to-own buyer ready to cash out, you can offer to cash-out the OF seller early in exchange for a discount. A 10 or 15 percent discount makes for a very profitable deal for the investor and is fair for the sellers because it's optional to take only if they want the cash now rather than waiting another year.

You as an investor must be comfortable with any OF terms because you are obligated to make payments on the home you bought or the seller can foreclose and take back the property. You've also got to be comfortable with how you prescreened your tenant-buyer in the home and make sure that buyer has enough down payment so they're not going to back out too easily. With all buyers, we evaluate their "skin in the game" by looking at the size and source of the down payment. For example, if the source was borrowed money, they could have less of a challenge walking away—defaulting on you—than if they used their own funds.

SUBJECT TO (ST)

In this bucket, a seller transfers the deed to the property to the investor *subject to the existing debt staying in place*. In other words, the seller's mortgage doesn't go away, it is not paid off or assumed by the investor, but remains in the seller's name. As an investor, you have agreed in writing to make payments on a home you now own to a loan that's still in the seller's name. As you can imagine, this bucket can sometimes be difficult for sellers to embrace if they don't know you. Yet we do several of these deals each year and they've been done for many years around the country. Banks can't stop a transfer of a deed.

One potentially cumbersome aspect of the sandwich lease is that when the lease-purchase term ends, which could be as long as nine years later, the investor has to track down the seller to sign over the deed. A strategy we have used after having a sandwich lease in place for about a year or so, having built up trust and credibility in the relationship by making our regular payments, is that we ask the seller to transfer the deed, moving the deal into the ST bucket. Sellers may agree because of the trust factor or because they want closure. We've done many where they are leaving the state and want to get the paperwork done first.

Earlier we discussed how every mortgage has a due-on-sale clause, in which the bank requires its loan be paid off before any transfer of the home. But a federal law, the Garn-St. Germain Depository Institutions Act of 1982, said a property can transfer to a family member or trust for estate-planning reasons without triggering the due-on-sale clause, so those kinds of transfers are happening regularly. In our experience, as long as banks are getting their payments, they are happy to take the checks and are not calling back any of the hundreds of loans in the ST transactions done by us, our partners, and the investors we coach. The risk for the seller lies in the investor not making payments.

The positives for you as an investor are:

- You have no deadline to exit the deal—no balloon payment due.

- You have full control of the property and can place your own insurance.

- You bought a home with no credit check, and the loan stayed in the seller's name.

- You don't have to chase the seller down years later to get a deed signed over.

- You write off taxes, interest, and depreciation as the owner of record.

WHOLESALE

When you, as an investor, take control of a property by way of any of the deals described previously and then assign your contract to another investor, that's the wholesale bucket. The other investor must fulfill the contract, while you pick up an assignment fee. It might range from $5,000 to $20,000, although that high end on larger homes is not too common. Some investors make a business out of wholesaling. We don't because we want ongoing cash flow, not small checks from one-payday transactions that we'd have to do again and again.

Though we don't look for these deals, we had one recently where the seller insisted on a cash purchase despite our offering a higher price through a different bucket. We put the home under contract with the full understanding that we were going to find someone to step into our shoes. As far as the seller was concerned, she had a cash sale that would happen on or before a specified date. We found a rehabber that does exactly these types of deals. The rehabber took over, and we received a $10,000 wholesale-assignment fee. It's one of the buckets you can use to exit a deal you're not comfortable with.

OPTIONING

Placing an option on a property is a simple one-page agreement with a seller to buy it at a certain price. Let's say you're contracting to buy a home at $200,000. You agree with the seller to pay a $100 nonrefundable fee for the option to have a 60-day or 90-day window to find a buyer, just like wholesaling, to step into your shoes to then close the contract.

You, as an investor, can use an option for privacy if you close on the property and then sell it as a separate transaction, since the seller won't see the details of the profit you're making. You close with the buyer and simultaneously cash out the seller. An alternative that we prefer is to discuss openly with the seller how you are engineering the transaction and why you need a notice of option recorded to protect your interest. Then the person taking over the option can close directly with the seller, and you will be paid an option-release fee that's not a surprise to the seller.

We option a property about once a year. It happens when we are very unclear what price we can get for the property, how fast we can get it, or because it's exceptionally high-end and we're just not sure how the market's going to react. We might put an option on it for 30 or 60 days and tell the seller we're going to take it to market and see what happens.

The wholesale and optioning buckets are very similar and are both alternatives for sellers who want cash right away and won't agree to the longer terms of the other buckets.

MINIMIZING INVESTOR RISK

Our business started with almost all AO deals, and now we do almost all SW and OF transactions. The AO deals carried less risk of our making mistakes because the lease-purchaser became the seller's responsibility. Over time we realized that in the SW deals, we could put away the monthly spread, Payday #2, in our reserve account. That covers us for the occasions when life happens to some tenants and collecting becomes a headache, once or twice a year out of our 50 or so deals. The legal components of our SW agreements allow us at any point in the term of a contract to assign that contract back to the seller without his or her consent, so there's no huge risk unless you didn't listen to me and made a down payment in the deal.

On an owner-financing deal, you as the investor have two ways to avoid foreclosure if you are not taking in the money necessary to cover your payments. You can renegotiate amicably with the seller, just as you would do in asking a bank for a loan modification. Or if they won't negotiate, you could deed the property back to the seller.

We haven't had to deal with that type of situation, but we make a practice of being proactive whenever we anticipate any problems with buyers.

While the choice of buckets depends on the seller's circumstances, we have seen that it also can benefit buyers, who are the subject of the next chapter.

chapter 6

OKAY, I HAVE THESE PROPERTIES, NOW WHAT DO I DO?

The first time a new transaction engineer takes control of a property, excitement mixes with anxiety over whether there's a buyer to be found. In fact, that's the easy part, even with homes where it would traditionally be difficult to find a buyer.

Imagine a house that sits next to a bar and used to have a business in it. We worked with a family that was relocating to the Philippines and needed to sell a house like that in Clinton, Massachusetts. It was in a residential area, and the bar had limited hours, but it was just not the prettiest home to market, nor was it the best location. When a buyer sets out to search for a home that can qualify for a loan, I don't think they say, "Hmmm, let's go see if we can find a home next to a bar." Still we found a lease-purchase buyer and earned Three Paydays: an $11,000 down payment, $350 net monthly cash flow, and $36,000 on the back end.

We even sold a home with a Joint-Venture Partner in Virginia that was barely habitable. It needed so much work that the average rehabber wouldn't touch it. But fairly quickly a buyer came forward and agreed to pay $69,900 through a lease-purchase. The Three Paydays were an $8,753 down payment, $250 net monthly cash flow, which totals $12,000 over four years, and the back-end cash-out of $37,756. So believe it or not, we earned $58,509 on a home that we bought for $48,700 and sold as-is. The sellers were out-of-state and we relieved them of worrying about the house being empty. The buyer was happy because he didn't have enough cash to buy the house outright but realized the upside value of fixing it up by doing the work himself.

A large pool of potential buyers is out there with no credit or bad credit. They feel there's no one willing to help them, to give them hope of home ownership. They see our ad or website, which says, "Buyers: no bank qualifying, no credit or bad credit—no problem. Rent-to-own your dream home." To help walk a potential buyer through the process, we have videos on our website to answer all their commonly asked questions. Most important, the videos make clear that we are not working with people who just want to rent. But if they prequalify themselves by watching the videos, they see we welcome their call, and when my son, Nick, talks to them, as our buyer specialist, it puts them at ease. He is an expert at what he does and he helps our new investors become experts.

The videos educate the buyers that we need a down payment of at least 3 percent, but we try to get them into the range of 5 to 10 percent when we talk with them. If they can put 10 percent down, we know we have someone strong. We call this down payment the first of our Three Paydays, but it can extend out over time as cash flow, if the investor is willing to take it in installments. We gladly take installments and have hundreds of thousands of dollars scheduled to come in each of the next two years. How would you feel ending this calendar year knowing that you have another $50,000 or $100,000 or more scheduled to come in? By the way, the videos mentioned here (Buyer Q&A), as well as all the Seller Q&A videos are all made available for your own website as a JV Partner!

When a prospective buyer has sufficient funds for the down payment or a plan to get there, we'll meet with him or her. But first, we require the buyer speak with a company that checks his or her credit and looks for any criminal record or history of sexual harassment. The vendor we use specializes in credit enhancement. He also used to be a mortgage broker, so he knows the underwriting rules and regulations, and he will talk with the buyer by phone, review credit history and personal situation, and tell us the pertinent information about when he or she will be what we call "mortgage ready." We put all of our tenant-buyers through this intensive but inexpensive screening—$50 per person, as of this writing. Then our agreements require them to participate in the credit-enhancement program, which is $99 per month per person for six months minimum to start out.

We'll be told, for example, that they can repair their credit in 9 to 12 months, 12 to 18 months, or 18 to 24 months, typically. Occasionally it goes up to three years, but that's rare. So most of our terms we're structuring give the buyer three years to get a mortgage, which provides a buffer from the time they should be credit-worthy and mortgage-ready.

We are almost always accepting or rejecting buyers purely on financial criteria, like a bank would. In coaching new investors, this is an important point, and they should familiarize themselves with antidiscrimination laws nationally and where they live. Our training videos explain what criteria we use and how we put that in writing for buyers we reject. We did have a seller who was doing an AO deal with us reject a buyer who recently had been in jail for a cocaine conviction; it showed on the criminal check, which is part of the screening.

On the other hand, we accepted a buyer recently who had one little ding on her criminal history. We chatted with her and decided we were comfortable that she had just been in the wrong place at the wrong time as a young teenager.

Before we make the final decision to accept buyers, they meet with us. We live in Rhode Island, the smallest state in the country, and on an island within Rhode Island, so we have to do business in a broader area across New England. Some of our buyers are as much as a two-hour drive away from us. But we've never found buyers, if they are serious, having any problem driving that distance to meet us or come to our attorney's office because they're so excited to have this program—and them meeting us is just as important as us needing or wanting to meet them.

At the meeting, we go over a "buyer letter of intent" they sign, that signifies they understand their down payment is not refundable if they're accepted, and they are taking the home as-is and accepting all responsibility. The letter says whether they are performing inspections or waiving them. If they are doing inspections, they understand we are keeping the home on the market in the meantime.

Because they are signing a lease, not closing on a home purchase, attorneys are not required by law to be present. But for clarity, and so they take it seriously, we treat it like a closing. We have them sign all the documents in front of our attorney after we accept them. This protects both parties.

They need to understand that, concerning possible repairs, it's just like they bought the home—that they can't call us about a clogged toilet or a leaky roof. An exception to their being just like a buyer is that they cannot buy a homeowner's insurance policy until the home is in their name, but they must buy a tenant policy, which is inexpensive. Whoever is on the deed pays for the homeowner's policy, but the buyer legally must fulfill any requirements of that policy, such as having smoke alarms.

TENANT-PROTECTION LAWS

Whether or not a lease-purchase buyer can take advantage of state tenant-protection laws to override the purchase-option language in our contracts is a gray area. Almost every lawyer I have asked said courts probably would find that the lease-purchase agreement can't force rent-to-own buyers to waive rights that they would otherwise have as a tenant. Frankly, we don't want to become the test case, so we try to fix any situation that comes up rather than have a judge decide our buyer has become our tenant.

Case in point: We had a family with four children move into a home we had bought subject to (ST) our paying the seller's loan. The seller disclosed no knowledge of lead paint, but the family did a home test, later confirmed, showing there was lead. Since the seller got out of the home under economic hardship, it fell to us to pay to mitigate the lead-paint hazard. That decision was right from a tenant-law standpoint. We could have dragged the family into court based on agreements our buyers sign that say they take the home as is, and our honest disclosure that we had no knowledge of lead, but morally, ethically, and legally we felt the right thing to do was to have the walls and woodwork stripped and repainted or covered over according to Massachusetts lead standards. That case caused us to update our agreements, putting the responsibility for any lead mitigation, mold, or asbestos back on the seller. If the seller has no money, however, what do you do? Well, you can avoid all this by doing proper inspections up-front on your end before deciding if you'd like to go forward.

WHEN LIFE HAPPENS

A buyer couple who were engaged when they signed the papers told us they had broken up and could not afford the home without both their incomes. They said, "We're sorry. Here are the keys back. We can't fulfill our obligation." We ended the deal amicably and retained their down payment.

Another buyer said, "My father-in-law had a second heart attack (way out of state in Chicago), and we're leaving, and here are the keys." Unfortunately, those life events come up once or twice a year to cut short multiyear deals. We refilled those homes with buyers who were stronger and had larger down payments. That can happen because our list of buyers grows over time as we market our homes, and sometimes we have multiple applicants for one home.

If a rent-to-own buyer is unable or unwilling to take out the mortgage to cash out a deal, he or she may ask to just stay as a tenant. Typically we give a nice 60- or 90-day notice to vacate and become someone else's tenant. For example, a couple who paid regularly asked to get out of a lease-purchase because they were expecting a child, unexpectedly. We said, "Just make sure you give us a 60-day notice, and we can refill the home." They were thrilled because they thought we were going to hold them to the years they had left in their lease and to a potential purchase. We had enough time before our balloon payment to the seller was due to simply put the home back on the rent-to-own market. If the due date were closer, we could have sold the home outright, still at a profit. But our analysis showed our profit would be far better by letting the term continue, as it was a good deal with principal-only monthly payments.

THE BUYER PROCESS IN DETAIL

Nick is our buyer specialist, so I asked him to describe in more detail the multiple layers of screening we use and show our members and partners how to implement. According to Nick:

> If you're a buyer and send an e-mail saying you want to look at a property, I'm going to send you a reply that's been carefully crafted and tested over the years to have the right language. We call it a "buyer-form" e-mail. That's going to direct you to the website and our Buyer Q&A videos, and only then, after you've seen the videos, can you call me to arrange a viewing.
>
> We place a lockbox on vacant homes so we can give a buyer a code for access. I'm very clear with all buyers that they are accountable and must confirm that they leave the house locked and the lockbox secure and let us know when they are in and out. When our sellers still occupy a home, they serve as our partner to walk the potential buyer through the home. I say "partner" because we have an equitable interest in all the properties that we have, and we're not real estate agents.
>
> Simultaneously to setting up that viewing, I'm going to e-mail the potential buyers our "Next Step" forms. I'm going to say to them, "After you view the home, if you are interested in taking the next step on this property, please fill out the forms and get them back to us." These forms have been crafted and tweaked over the years so they ask the right questions and give us the important things we need to know. They are also crafted to get the highest-pos-

sible down payment, which helps us but also puts them in a better position to get their financing at the end of the term. (Remember, we're setting people up to succeed.) After I get those forms back, I'll call the tenant-buyer to go over that information. My goal is clarity on where the payments are coming from. The forms we use list several sources—retirement accounts; tax refunds; and other assets, such as a car they might think about selling—to get the buyer thinking about where he or she could get money for a down payment.

Suppose it's going to take a buyer three years of credit repair to get to a point to be able to get a mortgage, and he or she expects a $10,000 tax refund every year. We'll see if that buyer would be comfortable committing, for example, $7,000 of that refund for three consecutive years. It's important at this stage to make sure the buyer is telling *you* a number, so that if there's ever a challenge paying, it's not a number you came up with. So in this example, by calling and speaking with the buyer in more depth, we're able to get an extra $21,000 out of that conversation (Payday #1 in installments).

If we come to a point where we're comfortable with a buyer's information, we're going to go ahead and schedule a meeting. As soon as it is booked, I arrange for the buyer to call the credit-repair specialist we work with. I let him or her know the specialist will in turn send him or her to a website to pay $50 for the tenant screening, but the call comes first because we like to have the human element involved so the buyer doesn't feel like he or she is buying a house through a computer.

Our first concern with tenant-buyers is not that they don't have money for the down payment but *how long* it's going to take them to be mortgage-ready. And it's from the tenant screening that we're able to see this. All the dates in any agreement that we have with them will be based on how long it's going to take them to be approved for a loan. The buyers pay for their own screening. When it results in them getting a home, they are more than happy about it. These are people with good incomes and money saved for a down payment who still could not get a loan for one reason or another. At closings, I hear, "Thank God we found you guys. We didn't feel like there was a way out. We felt like we were trapped." We're providing a path to home ownership.

Sometimes our prospective buyers start off the first call with me by saying something like, "Yeah, yeah, I don't need credit repair" or, "My credit's great." I say, "Oh, okay. Great. You can get a loan today," and then they reveal they need more time on the job or time for something to come off their credit report. The truth always comes out once you are on the phone with buyers, and as soon as they understand we're there to help and that they're just like everyone else, their guard comes down. A common misconception is with the word "credit." It doesn't refer to just their credit score. What we're referring to goes deeper and refers to their whole profile as buyers. Sometimes when we say "credit repair" to buyers, a defensive wall goes up. We like the phrase "credit enhancement" instead.

TESTIMONIALS FROM BUYERS

"Pre Property Solutions made our experience of getting into a home easy and hassle free. They were there to answer any questions we may have had and made the experience very positive. We got into our home within a few weeks and they went above and beyond—truly an amazing group of people. Thank you Pre Property Solutions for getting us into a lovely home!"

"We had such a great experience with Pre Property Solutions! We found a home and were able to finish the process and get in the house in as little as three weeks! We are with our kids snuggled on the couch in our new living room, grateful for everything they've done to make having a home possible!"

—Jason and Kristin V.

"After a divorce and hitting roadblock after roadblock when trying to buy a new house, I was referred to Pre Property Solutions by my brother-in-law, who stated they were great to work with. I contacted Chris and began the process. Once I found a house, everything moved quickly and smoothly. Chris, Nick, and Susan not only answered all my questions but did so in a very timely manner. They made the process easy and stress free. I think the biggest thing for me was that I was not made to feel guilty because of my credit status. Instead, I was assured that many people are in my position and the thought of owning another home was not impossible but more probable and attainable. I would and

will definitely recommend Pre Property Solutions to friends and family. It has always been my dream to buy a big, old Victorian home and restore her to her original beauty, and because of Pre Property Solutions I am now living my dream."

"My husband and I were stuck. We owned a property that we couldn't immediately get out of, for many reasons. This caused us to not only be forced to become landlords, as the townhouse no longer met our needs with one-year-old twins but also to move twice in three short years. We wanted so much to settle into a community that our children would grow up in. We came across Pre Property Solutions when searching for yet another rental. We called and spoke with them, and I found myself excited and scared all at the same time! Could this be real? Very skeptical, but curious, we pursued this home, and we are so happy we did! Chris and team made it happen for us! They held my hand through the entire process. They worked within our particular situation, and it happens fast! We will be moving into our beautiful new home, within a fabulous school district, next week! More than that, Chris bought our townhouse with their lease to own only weeks after we signed on our own property! He set it up so that the timing for purchase, on both ends, works perfectly for us. I'm guessing that, as you read this, you'll find yourself very skeptical, as we were. My only advice is to take the time to check it out and talk with Chris. You won't be disappointed!"

MARKETING TECHNIQUES

We provide our members a checklist to walk them through how to properly market a property. Of course, we put a listing on the website, post to online classified services and social media, and e-mail a list of buyers. Our coaching shows members how to make that list and how to implement or replicate a version of the videos that Nick referred to. Our Joint-Venture Partners can choose between us providing them a done-for-you set of videos or making their own using our video scripts.

I tell new investors, "It may sound trivial, but get associated with your chamber of commerce, and get associated with your Better Business Bureau immediately because people are checking that right away." I joined both organizations after an incident in 2013. One Saturday morning I sat in my office waiting for a buyer who was driving 90 minutes to see me and had even confirmed by phone that he was on the way. Eventually the buyer's uncle, an attorney, called saying, "I checked online and you're not even a member of the chamber of commerce or Better Business Bureau." He had told his nephew he suspected a scam and not to bring me a check. Thanks to that wacko call, we have been an A or A+ rating accredited member ever since. I want to thank those people who throw curveballs at us because it sometimes helps us improve our business.

We have experimented in our marketing with different business models within the real estate field. For several years we bought properties near colleges, either conventional or on terms, and rented them only to college students, whose parents cosigned. It was very profitable; the properties paid themselves down, allowing us to exit with a conventional sale over time.

We also recently released training information for our members on land-only deals using the same terms we use for homes. Some people want to build a home but don't know how to begin or can't get the conventional financing that requires 50 percent down on the land. We are partnering with builders to offer what becomes a finished product. That business model opens up a new buyer pool and profit center.

In our Joint-Venture Partnerships, we offer an exclusive territory, perhaps three or four counties, where nobody else from our team or other JV Partners will be competing. If someone else has been in the market teaching or practicing sales on terms, our attitude is that there's still plenty of business out there. Some of the strategies we use have been around long before we started, but we are constantly evolving the strategies and setting up the systems to support our business based on actually doing deals—not just teaching about them.

In dealing with our buyers, we live and learn, just as we do with our sellers. So every time we have a challenge, we tweak the system to handle that, and our new investors have access to those improvements, which is invaluable. In the next chapter we explain why we can say our systems are proven and predictable.

chapter 7

SIMPLE, PROVEN, PREDICTABLE, AND PROFITABLE WITH THE RIGHT COACH

I have referred several times to my coaching new investors. This chapter will explain in detail how that coaching works, how it provides investors a simple, proven, predictable, and profitable game plan.

But being coachable involves a lot more than signing up for a program. Being a transaction engineer requires not only learning types of deals but also developing the right work habits. To help you understand what I mean, let's go back to where the book began, the 2008 debacle when we were out of money and dealing with multiple property foreclosures. We got back on track to success using five techniques that I will share with you here.

1. THE RIGHT COACH

The first way we were able to reengineer our business was by finding someone who already had done exactly what we were thinking of doing. We identified the path we wanted to take and then connected with someone who could lead us with mentoring and coaching.

The mentor would have to be alongside us to provide the emotional strength one needs to succeed in any business and also feedback to keep us on the right path. Anyone attaining outstanding achievements must have motivation and persistence—but it takes coaches and mentors to keep a successful individual on track.

I'm not sure how many of you reading this book have coaches, or have even thought about having one. Since I got into real estate in 1995, I have had a coach, sometimes even two or three at a time, because different coaches can combine personal, physical, nutritional, and business and marketing guidance. I don't remember a time since 1995 when I wasn't paying from $200 to $2,000 a month for particular mentorship programs. Even while still rebuilding my business, I was part of an eight-person **mastermind group** in 2015 that cost $25,000 for three meetings yearly. That may seem crazy to some readers, but I can directly attribute well over $100,000 in income to those meetings. My reality is that proper associations enable us to learn and profit in the multimillions of dollars.

MASTERMIND GROUP:

A group of people with like-minded goals who support each other and keep each other accountable in developing their personal and business skills. The concept is that putting two or more minds together will exceed the productivity of the number participating because of the ideas that flow from the interaction. The concept has roots in one of the all-time best-selling business books, Think and Grow Rich *by Napoleon Hill (1937).*

When choosing a mentor, make sure that person has some history of success and is not just speaking and writing but actually doing what you want to do every day. I've looked back at my coaches and realized that many of them had some failures in their businesses—but those setbacks significantly strengthened their ability to succeed. And obviously that improves their ability to coach and help others succeed.

2. THE IMPORTANCE OF DISCIPLINE

We always told our kids growing up that with the right discipline, they could be outstanding at anything they wanted, whether that be school or work. So, the question is what new disciplines could you start acting on to improve your business or your life? With daily disciplines, an idea we introduced in chapter 4, you can improve every single day because what you do today has a direct relationship with the results you get tomorrow.

The dictionary definition of discipline is an activity, exercise, or regimen that develops or improves a skill. But here we are referring more specifically to the things you know you should be doing daily—even when you don't feel like it, and even when you don't see immediate results. Among successful people, not just in real estate but elsewhere, the common factor is that they form daily disciplines that people who fail don't like to practice. In our business, one daily discipline can be keeping a chart of calls made to prospects each day, or whatever might support your goal or fit into your Business Game Plan. We help you develop disciplines that will support your goals.

Reading and working on your mind can be a daily discipline, but too often the people I coach make it a goal that is too daunting. They say something like, "I'm going to read a book a month." But if it has been months since they read a book, they should start with a simple step like, "I'm going to read five minutes a day" and then start to raise the bar as they move along.

Another idea is to keep a journal and answer these three questions at the end of each day:

1. "What's the best thing that happened today?"

2. "What was the most challenging thing that happened today?"

3. "How can I improve tomorrow?"

By doing this, we're constantly working on disciplines, inching forward in short steps. Too few people realize how success is within their reach, but they're just not there yet mentally. Your success will be determined by your daily agenda. It's that simple. Forming new disciplines and habits may sound like a lot of work; however, it sure is a lot easier than letting all kinds of things you didn't do accumulate and then trying to tackle them all at once. Don't be looking back at what you should have done and be "shoulding" all over yourself, as Tony Robbins, the best-selling author and business strategist, likes to say. Instead, as a result of your new daily disciplines, you can say, "I'm so glad I did that."

3. CREATING MORE TIME IN YOUR DAY

Here in no particular order are ten ways to create more time in your day:

1. Literally buy time by hiring people to do things for you. This is the same as we explained in chapter 2 about getting a great rate of return by using personal assistants or adding team members.

2. Outsource tasks to vendors when you can pay someone much less than what your time is worth and you also know the return on investment is three to ten times what you're paying. If you think about your income—or income goals—in annual sums, figure out what it comes to per month, week, and hour. Everyone figures it a little differently, depending on how much time they plan to take

off during a given year. Someone earning $100,000 a year is making about $50 an hour based on eight-hour days. Considering no one can do high-payoff activities every hour of every day, any wasted high-value hours could easily cost $150.

3. Every night spend 15 minutes planning, and jot down five or six priority items for the next day. This activity does wonders, helping put your subconscious to work and clearing your mind so you can sleep calmly. You'll come to work fresh and you will stay focused all day.

4. If you want something done, block out time on your calendar. Make an appointment to do your daily disciplines and high-payoff activities. If you know you have to make three calls, treat it like a doctor's appointment and don't let anything else interfere. It's an appointment with yourself, and it's the most important one you can have. If someone asks you to be somewhere or do something and you know you have your time blocked out to make calls, tell them you're booked. When you are doing outgoing calls it is not a time to accept incoming calls. Figuratively speaking, you close the chamber door and don't open it until you've completed that task or appointment. When time blocking, you're working in sealed-off chambers.

5. Create a schedule you actually enjoy—one that you love. Don't be afraid to modify it every single month. We do that as a team. Every month we meet and see what can be tweaked. For example, I'm most effective at calling people in the morning. My son-in-law, Zach, puts most of his calls in the late afternoon. That's what works for him.

Your schedule also should support your goals. Once you establish your goals, we can help you establish a precise schedule that will get them done. That's why we call the program predictable.

6. Work like you're going on vacation tomorrow. It's a neat exercise to try because we get a whole bunch more done right before we go away, whether it is for business or pleasure. Imagine how much you would get done if I called you on a Sunday and said, "We're leaving tomorrow morning for Grand Cayman and you've got to be ready." As I write this, I am working feverishly and efficiently because I know I'm leaving for a trip. By the way, you know you have a business and not a job when you actually can go away and things continue with or without you. When we go to Grand Cayman for two or three weeks at a time, we totally shut down. I hope you're planning at least a few getaways every year. Heck, it's only one deal or so per year.

7. A simple but very effective technique over time is to go to bed earlier so you can get up earlier. One half-hour times 220 workdays equals 110 hours, or almost three workweeks a year you just created. How about if you give half of those hours to your family and half to your business?

8. Spend 80 percent of your time on marketing, prospecting, and other activities to create business and only 20 percent on servicing and minutiae. To accomplish this, you must track what you do during the week, a scary exercise that may show you are not necessarily doing what any business must do to grow—high-payoff activities.

9. Start your week on Sunday night by planning the entire week, as my team does. You'll be able to prioritize and get off to a better start Monday morning, a time many people waste because it takes them until the afternoon to reset.

10. Start your month by planning it out. A couple days prior to month's end but certainly no later than the last day of the month, look at the activities ahead, set your expectations, and set your checkpoints and *accountability*, which is the next issue we'll discuss. Every month as a team, we meet to discuss the months' results and any necessary adjustments needed, and then we set goals for the following month. Those are then followed up and tracked at our weekly huddle sessions.

4. CREATING MORE ACCOUNTABILITY

Regardless of what stage you're at in business, you can take steps to create more accountability. Here are ten ideas:

1. Even if you have no boss because you work for yourself, you can be accountable to your family or significant other. When our kids were younger, we'd promise them rewards based on our business calls per day. You can bet that if you promise kids a trip or vacation based on your call goal, they'll be asking you each day whether you made your calls.

2. Start every day at zero. If your goal is to make three calls a day, the count should start at zero regardless of whether you exceeded or fell short of the goal the previous day. By not gloating on your success the day before or getting upset if you weren't successful, you start fresh, strong, and undistracted.

3. Display a chart. If your goals are on a chart in your home or office, your family or office partners are going to ask you about it. As in #1, you are "going public" with your goals, which puts powerful emotion behind them. Just be careful going public with those that may not be in support of where you're headed.

4. Pay your assistant—or if you don't have an assistant, pay someone else—if you don't do certain tasks you said you were going to do. This accountability is particularly effective for lead generation or prospecting when you're early on in your business. Years ago as a real estate brokerage, we had a goal of calling 125 people every day, and we'd have to pay our assistant $10 or $25 if we failed. We also had a mastermind group back then in which we'd set monthly goals together and have to pay an assistant or accountability partner if goals were not achieved.

5. Let someone shadow you. You will tend to perform better when someone is watching you. We have people visit our office all the time from different parts of the country, and even before they arrive, their visits make us more efficient because we're busy setting up a day for them to see us at our best. How about if I flew into your market and shadowed you? You'd be surprised at what you'd get accomplished.

6. Pay your coach. I've already covered why having a coach is so important that I have never *not* had one. When you pay someone $1,000 or $2,000 a month for mentorship, you're not only going to listen to what he or she says but be accountable for getting it done.

7. Post your hourly income. Earlier in the chapter we discussed comparing the cost of an assistant to your own hourly income or income goal. I even suggest writing your hourly income on an index card posted at your desk. Do you think it would help you stay on task—to focus on work that moves you closer to your goal—if you had a sign in front of you saying what that work should be paying you? It absolutely does. You can use hourly, daily, weekly or monthly figures—whatever motivates and keeps you on task most effectively.

8. Post your schedule and tell everyone about it. Similar to posting your income goal, the visual cue will do wonders for your efficiency and accountability.

9. Find accountability partners. The eight partners from our mastermind group would call each other weekly or monthly to report our goals and results. I had a different accountability partner, who happened to be an attorney, just for book-reading goals. We would check in every month about whether or not we had done our reading. With other partners, we'd discuss our monthly deals and why or why not those goals were achieved and whether or not we were still committed to them.

10. Put yourself in a situation where you really don't have a choice. When we reengineered the business, I could have gone out and done some other things to earn money while building the real estate terms business. Instead we jumped full force into our own business with a mentor. The "burn-your-ships" concept refers to the 16th century Spanish explorer who burned his ships upon arrival in the New

World to send a message to his men that they could not turn back. It's great for me to coach someone who starts by saying, "I'm going to give this all I've got" and is prepared to leave a current job by a certain date. Don't get me wrong; I don't want you burning your ships before we have a plan in place and deals getting done. We can, however, get you there by a predictable date.

5. THE IMPORTANCE OF PERSISTENCE

It took years for you to become the person you are, and you can't change overnight. You *can* change anything you want over time, but if you're 30 years old, for example, please realize it took you 30 years to form your habits, positive and negative. So, please be persistent in your efforts to change, but be patient with yourself.

Let's say I'm coaching you, and you are doing everything in your game plan that we structured for your business and you're doing everything consistently in your personal plan. Success really is just a matter of time, and lack of patience and persistence is the biggest enemy to success. I'll see people come out of the gate strong, with everything lining up perfectly—but then they beat themselves up because success doesn't come quickly enough. Every business is going to take longer than one expects to become profitable. Here's an example: We teach you the exact number of leads you need per deal. You then go out and get those leads in the first month—then quit because a deal wasn't done. You need time to build up those leads and build up the funnel we talk about next—you need persistence and patience.

The marketing and sales process is often visualized as a funnel. When I'm coaching, I compare it to a funnel that is going to eventually have some oil go through it. When you pour oil into a dry funnel, it takes some time for it to coat the sides, but eventually, it flows much more smoothly and quickly. When you're collecting leads and filling out property-information sheets, you're "coating the sides," and in time, some high-quality prospects will pop out of the bottom of the funnel.

Persistence involves applying what you are learning—in this book or with a coach—every day, at every chance you get. Take your old ways and liken them to a spot right in front of you; draw an imaginary line in the sand, and step over it. As a coach once explained to me, at each stage of your personal and business growth, what got you to that point will hold you back from getting to the next level.

However, you can get there with the right coach, discipline, creating more time in your day, and creating more accountability. We're here to help you get that accomplished.

HOW WE CAN HELP

Home study: In addition to this book, we have a free eBook, *Eat That Sandwich—Creating Cash Flow Now, Continuous Cash Flow and Wealth*. On our website you can also download our special report on lead generation titled *Gather Your Nuts*. We currently have a free content-rich webinar running three or four times a week. We have a course that specializes in helping investors learn how to capture some profits on land that they drive past daily. We have a full *Quantum*

Leap Systems (QLS) Course, which has 15 or more videos and a full downloadable transcription of each video for your reference. These can all be found on the website and serve as a great starting place or prelude to the full coaching or JV Partnership.

---

www.SmartRealEstateCoach.com

Membership: We invite those interested in tapping into our systems, coaching and necessary forms and checklists to become members. There is a fourteen-day trial membership or one- and three-year discounted memberships available. Our higher-level partnerships require membership, which is generally paid on a discounted yearly or three-year basis. Our personal coaching involves our ACAA (Action, Critique, Adjust, Action) approach, discussed in chapter 4.

Mastermind group: The group discussion occurs by phone once a week for eight weeks. This is FREE for our JV Partners. The cost as of this writing is $999. Imagine interacting every week with our JV Partners—discussing deals, challenges, best ways to succeed, and more.

To give you an example of how well this works, we were discussing in the mastermind group recently how to increase the average down payment from the buyers (Payday #1) so that they are in a much better position when it comes time for financing. A member from Las Vegas acknowledged that he was having a tough time getting the checks that he kept hearing us talk about. In the discussion, a couple of us thought of asking him whether he had discussed with buyers whether they had a 401(k) or other retirement plan funds that they could tap into for a home purchase. He didn't realize they could do that for a rent-to-own down payment. The following week, he asked a buyer that simple question—and as a result, got a much higher down payment from a buyer who otherwise would not have had the cash to even qualify for the program. That investor had already gotten more than his money's worth from the cost of joining the group.

JV Club: Our newest addition, JV Club is the lowest-level JV program and involves a different split with us but allows more members to easily participate. For more on JV Club membership, visit the Membership Levels section on our website.

The next four levels are more expensive (see website for current pricing), They are:

1. We offer six months of consulting and coaching.

2. Our Joint-Venture (JV) Starter Program requires a deposit that the partners earn back on their first four or five deals.

3. The 5-Day Immersion JV Program includes myself and/ or team members flying or driving into your market. We produce leads and set up appointments with you and your sellers before coming and actually doing deals and meeting with sellers and buyers while we're in your marketplace, guaranteeing you a set number of deals. You can see the website for details, but it also includes free admission to our yearly event, free yearly mastermind sessions with other partners, free coaching, and more. This and the next program are a complete no-brainer decision based on return on investment in the program and are for the more

serious individuals. If you're looking for the fastest path to success, these more aggressive programs are best for you, and participation is limited. You can apply to see if you are a fit and if your area is still available.

4. The High-6-Figure JV Protected Area Program includes the 5-Day Immersion Program, but with multiple trips by our team to the market, a protected geographic area in which we place no other partners, more guaranteed deals, more leads we generate before coming out, two full years of unlimited coaching, and more.

Let's think about this and recap for a minute. Earlier in the book, I showed how the Three Paydays typically provide profits of approximately $65,000. The JV Programs guarantee deals. Is there anything to really hold you back? Any business, franchise, or other cash-generating vehicle with that type of return and minimum overhead usually carries higher price tags and fees (franchises anywhere from $35,000–$1 million and more with overrides and lifetime fees). We're not with you for life unless you want us to be. We're capped at what we earn with you and then you're 100 percent profiting on your own.

Joint-Venture Partners have access to all of our resources—not only online but also all of our team members. Many of the JV Partners also use vendors that we have selected through trial and error and use the experienced-virtual-assistant service we already have trained to generate our leads.

FINDING YOUR LEVEL

As members study with us, at whichever membership level or JV Coaching Level they choose, I see the light bulb go off once they understand how these deals are predictable. They realize that yes, they can do them, but that they want to shorten the learning curve dramatically by having us in the trenches with them through one of the three Joint-Venture Partnership programs.

Obviously, everybody is going to have different results, but those programs guarantee that deals will happen quickly. When JV Partners are calling sellers and eventually buyers, they can lean on our 25-plus years of experience in the real estate business. They can lean on our credibility with the Better Business Bureau, the longevity of our company, and the exposure of our website. That's a big advantage, especially in their first year in business.

BUILDING CASH FLOW AND WEALTH

While the ability to generate cash flow and build wealth as a transaction engineer is predictable, it's also unlimited. Since all deals are made on YOUR TERMS, you don't "need" to take on anything that you're not comfortable with. That means you don't have to work with any pain-in-the-butt sellers, and you can turn off the flow through the funnel at any point. If you already have booked enough paydays to meet your needs, you can take a year off or retire. As of this writing, we have hundreds of thousands of Payday #1 dollars scheduled to come in next year and again the year after that. We also have several million Payday #3 dollars scheduled to come in over the next three to six years. Our present monthly Payday #2s more than cover all of our overhead, and we'll show you how to do the same. That is not to impress you but rather to impress *upon* you that YOU can have total control over when, how, and how much you work, when you want to relax and travel with your family, and how much wealth you want to retire with.

As we reengineered our business after the 2008 debacle, my wife and I simultaneously, consciously, and drastically reduced our personal overhead. We owned too many homes and have since reduced that cost by about 80 percent or more than $45,000 a month. Without that financial pressure, we could make deals that we found fun and profitable, rather than feeling a need to take on just any deal.

We go into a deal figuring out how to structure it to meet the needs of both the seller and the buyer. But then there are some decisions we make on OUR TERMS. This might involve nudging the buyer along toward a cash-out, for example, if we need more cash flow this year, this month, or this quarter. The deal could be structured from the start to allow for accelerating our Payday #3 if we know that would help us with a financial commitment. For some readers, that could be putting a child through college. Recently we had a buyer call us ready to cash out two years early, so we went back to the seller and renegotiated a little discount for ourselves in exchange for the earlier payout. Small adjustment techniques like this will add tens of thousands to your bank account—per deal!

The cash-out from buyers is usually predictable because of their prequalification to have their credit up to standards before our exit date. So, we're always setting them up to succeed. Still, we check in with them to make sure they're going to be mortgage ready, and we walk them through that process. Delaying a cash-out for a buyer might even make sense for an investor who wants to put off the income into the next year for tax-saving purposes.

With good work habits—discipline, more time, accountability, persistence, and the right coaching—you can have a business in which you structure simple, proven, predictable, and profitable deals to suit buyers, sellers, and your needs. Still, some deals should simply be avoided, as you'll see in the next chapter.

chapter 8

WHAT COULD GO WRONG?

On a cold New England night in late September 2000, I got a call at two o'clock a.m. from one of my business partners in a set of rental property holdings near Holy Cross College in Worcester, Massachusetts. He said raw sewage was a foot deep in the basement of one of the homes. To head off a board of health condemnation that would displace our college-student tenants, we had to go over there and handle that cleanup ourselves, not a pleasant task. (Nowadays, a management company handles our multifamily properties and deals with calls like these.) We discovered only after a repeat incident that tree roots had grown into the sewer line and caused a backup, the kind of problem you can't plan for.

Today, we no longer hold rental properties bought the traditional way with down payments and loans and no longer deal with many of the headaches associated with tenants, but that particular sewage problem could bite anyone in any country with any property, whether it's rent-to-own or not.

WHAT OTHER GURUS REFUSE TO TELL YOU

This chapter covers a variety of issues with properties, tenants, contracts, and deal terms that most investors will never face but should know about anyway. Luckily, most challenges that we've had, we've created systems for. These systems could be as simple as a checklist that we use in our office or during a property walkthrough. We've also made additions and changes to our standard legal agreements with the help of our attorney to safeguard against situations we encountered—problems other gurus in our field refuse to even tell you about.

Some of the other mentors or coaches in our industry have told me point-blank that they won't talk about possible pitfalls with any particular techniques that they're teaching because they don't want to scare away any potential audience. I believe that if I don't teach you about what we've learned could go wrong, you might encounter those pitfalls and be upset that we didn't share them with you.

Frankly, some of the other mentors and coaches may not actually be aware of current challenges, because they no longer do enough deals themselves. Experience in the field is necessary because the industry changes rapidly, and we've got to change with the market, laws, and regulations. Because we are out in the field doing four to six or more deals per month, we are going to run into almost anything one can run into and pass along that information to our members.

Our agreements with sellers allow us to do a full inspection and to back away if we want to. Even when we are passing on the home and any potential headaches to the tenant-buyer, we might as well know up-front if something has to be done and have the seller address that so we don't have that come back and bite us if our buyer should default.

LIFE EVENTS WILL HAPPEN

Aside from property problems, we have to deal with people's life events. One of our rent-to-own buyers was diagnosed with stage IV cancer and needed to find a place to live closer to her Boston hospital. What we said was, "No problem. You take your time. You go through your treatments. You can become just a standard tenant of ours, and when the time is right for you and when you've found a place closer to your hospital, you can go ahead and move out. And just give us some notice, so that we can go ahead and resell the home." She was thrilled. We're fine. We're collecting a monthly check and eventually will fill the home with another tenant-buyer and collect another Payday #1 deposit. Meanwhile, the principal on the underlying mortgage in the sellers' name is being paid down monthly.

One of our best tenant-buyers, who worked in an auto body shop, got pinned against a wall by a car and was out of work for a while. We were not going to kick the family out, although they couldn't afford the payments. We said, "Look, things happen. You're going to pay more to leave us and move than you are if we just lower your rent and weather the storm with you, and then when you're back on your feet, you can get back on your payment schedule." It was a win-win because we collected a reduced rent for six months rather than having an empty house, money that covered the underlying mortgage payment. It was winter, and nobody wants to move during the winter and during the holidays. Good communications saved them and us headaches.

Another tenant-buyer became disabled and had to leave the home, so we refilled it. These extreme life events affect perhaps one deal a year out of around 50 deals. In most cases we find even stronger buyers and get better down payments because our prescreening improves with experience.

We have seen new investors rushing to get a buyer and skipping our recommended prescreening by a credit-enhancement company that also checks criminal and sexual-harassment records. That can be a major pitfall. We've learned that if buyers are not properly pre-screened to figure out when they will be mortgage-ready, and if they have not put down a large enough down payment, they are nothing more than tenants. A tenant can get into a home in most states by paying the first and last month's rent and a security deposit. If that's the size of a buyer's down payment, all you have is a tenant who could easily default. *Don't* accept that. Follow the systems and guidelines we've outlined, and you'll be happy, as will your bank account.

THE "LIGHTER" ISSUES FROM OUR CLIENTS

As in any business, we hear concerns or excuses that we don't want to turn into stumbling blocks. If a Joint-Venture Partner claims to be unable to find an attorney, we have referral sources, and for the higher-level JV programs, our attorney will speak with your potential attorney in your area. If potential JV Partners say they are intimidated by the paperwork, we have the few necessary agreements and forms predone and packaged in our membership area. Since 2005, about $200,000 and many hundreds of hours have gone into preparation of our resources and education. If JV Partners need help finding sellers, we share our assistants, who are trained at generating leads.

We often get asked by new investors, "What if the market drops suddenly?" All of our deal structures involve significant monthly principal paydown, which protects against any downturn in the market. But the reality is that, at any point, the transaction engineer can go back to the seller and renegotiate. As explained in chapter 5, the investor is not personally on the hook for any loan and retains the right to assign the lease-purchase agreement back to the seller, who in most cases doesn't want it back.

BUYERS' TROUBLE GETTING A MORTGAGE

When it comes time for rent-to-own buyers to get a mortgage, we've seen two extremes: Some buyers call two years ahead of schedule and say, "We're cashing this home out," and that's a great surprise. On the other hand, occasionally we get a call from someone whose credit has improved, but not by enough for them to meet their deadline to get a mortgage at a rate they consider affordable. In the latter case, we have gone back to the seller and said, "Look, I know we had a cash-out coming up, but the buyer is super-close and working really hard." And we ask for a three- or a six-month extension or more. It has happened twice this year (2016), and both times the sellers agreed because they had been getting paid regularly each month and were super happy with us.

THE BOTTOM LINE

Our business begins with the premise that we are not risking our own money in making deals on OUR TERMS. But as you have seen in this chapter, things can come up a year or more into a deal—a legal bill, a repair—that will cost some money. In our opinion, prudent business sense requires keeping a reserve fund, to which we dedicate most of our Payday #2s, the monthly spread between what we're paying a mortgage company or a seller and the income we're getting from our tenant-buyers. When a curveball gets thrown our way, we don't have to panic, because we have that reserve. You should also put a portion of your Payday #1s into a savings account. With all our entities, we use approximately 2.5 percent. You won't miss it on a deal and you'll rest easy knowing it's in reserves.

There is nobody in our business, including any mentor I've ever paid myself, who doesn't get hit by those curveballs—because of two facts about the real estate market: It is forever changing, and more important, real estate is dealing with *people*, their unpredictable behavior, and life events. So, we won't ever claim to have it all "figured out," but you've seen in this chapter how we use communication and problem solving to evolve the program that we teach our members and partners. We've been up-front about what can go wrong, but the next chapter spotlights how great this business is most of the time—not only because of the profits waiting for you but also the tears of joy you see when you help buyers fulfill their dream of a home of their own.

chapter 9

DESIGN YOUR LIFESTYLE

The deal I am about to describe is not something that happens to a new investor every month, so I don't want you to get that idea. With patience and persistence, a transaction engineer eventually will run into sellers who are amazingly easy to deal with, ready to sign papers, and able to walk away happy. We had a case in which one phone call resulted in two deals and instant cash flow.

The lead source was expired listings, homes that had languished after being listed with a real estate agent. We called the owners of the property in Connecticut and found out they were moving to Florida. An out-of-state move at the end of an expired listing makes for a motivated seller—one of my favorite when I see that on the property information sheet. The property was a duplex, two attached single-family homes, which in this zoning jurisdiction have to be considered separate condominiums. The property was built in the 1990s, sparing us any structural or lead-paint issues. The only reason we could think of why the property did not sell on the open market was a steep driveway.

We were looking at a deal in which the seller would vacate one condo, which we could fill with a tenant-buyer, and assign us the lease of the tenant who was in the other condo. We generally do not want to become landlords, but in this case we were comfortable doing so temporarily. My son-in-law met with the seller's tenant/neighbor and found a highly disciplined military man who had been paying his rent a couple days early each month. His lease with the seller was expiring in about eight months, at which time we could renew, convert him into a tenant-buyer, or not renew and fill the property with another rent-to-own buyer.

About ten days after we took control of the two condos, we received our first rent from the existing tenant, about $460 more than we had to pay out for the mortgage. That's immediate cash flow. Within 30 days, the other unit, which was just made vacant with the sellers' move, sold to a great military family on a lease-purchase term of three years—more than enough time for their necessary credit enhancement. That family began paying us about $1,550 per month, which gave us a spread of almost $600 after we paid the mortgage, so now our total cash flow was $1,059.57 per month on these two attached units. One phone call to a seller with an expired listing resulted in a profit of almost $90,000 even before doing anything further with the rental side.

TRANSACTION ENGINEER SUMMARY SHEET

SOURCE OF LEAD: EXPIRED LISTING CALL-IN HOUSE

PURCHASE PRICE: (A) $115,811 MORTGAGE PLUS $36,000 CASH TO SELLER AT END OF TERM

(B) $127,457 MORTGAGE PLUS $24,546 CASH TO SELLER AT END OF TERM

BUCKET: SW (SANDWICH LEASE-PURCHASE)

MONTHLY PAYMENT OUT: (A) $939.72 (B) $951

PAYMENT TYPE: DIRECT TO MORTGAGE COMPANY

BUYER TERM: (A AND B) 36 MONTHS

SELL PRICE: (A) DEFERRED FOR EXISTING TENANTS
(B) SOLD FOR $184,900

MONTHLY LEASE IN: (A) $1,400 (B) $1,550.19

SELL TERM: 36 MONTHS

PAYDAY #1 DOWN PAYMENT FOR UNIT B
$21,000   ONE-TIME

PAYDAY #2 RENT FOR B MINUS MORTGAGE
$21,571   SPREAD OVER 36 MONTHS

PAYDAY #3 CASH-OUT FROM SALE OF B*
$43,900   AT END OF DEAL

TOTAL : $86,471

*Payday #3 is calculated this way: Unit B sale price is $184,900. Subtract $24,546 cash-out to seller and $127,457 paid directly to mortgage company over 36 months. There is $32,897 left, but add back in about $11,000 in equity gained by paying down principal for those 36 months.

WHO CAN MAKE THIS WORK?

In our training and mentoring, we encounter four types of people:

1.   There are people who see the potential but lack the confidence to start even a home-study course. I suggest they speak with me in a free, 15-minute strategy session, which I will do for any reader of this book who requests it. We can work out the roadblocks, which are mostly self-imposed, and they will have some great takeaways, whether or not they choose to work with us.

2.   Other people understand the possibilities but are hesitant to devote any financial resources. I ask them to pretend they're seeing me on stage at a seminar, and I ask the audience, "How many can reach in their pocket and pull out a $100 bill right now?" Most wouldn't have that. But what if I said, "I will give everybody in the room five hours to go out and secure a $100 bill, and those who do, come to the front of the room and receive a matching $100." A guaranteed 100 percent return on your money would make you resourceful enough to go out and get that $100 bill. We have suggestions online including not just going to relatives or friends but discovering how to find a business line of credit company and how to finance with us.

3. Some people see the potential, have the confidence, and gather the resources, but they unrealistically expect immediate results. We teach that it might take going through as many as 35 leads to get a cash-in-hand deal. The people we're speaking of here go through 35 leads, and then they throw their arms up, and say, "Well, this didn't work for me." But with their funnel of leads filling up, if they simply gave it more time, it would work.

4. The more mature entrepreneurs we deal with have the confidence, find the resources, and display the patience to develop a successful business. They understand that some businesses aren't even profitable after two or three years. This business can potentially be profitable within the first six months and sometimes the first 60 days. As a result, they join the higher-level JV Programs and have huge success, like some you have seen in this book and on our site under Testimonials. I refer to these people as being *Fully Positioned* with us.

So, those who can take our training, manage expectations, and give themselves six months or so to see the results can run this path with us quite successfully.

CONSIDER THE ALTERNATIVES

Some people spend $35,000 to $1 million to buy a franchise that's probably not going to be profitable for a few years. They also are likely with a franchise to have a huge monthly overhead. You've seen how our type of business can cost a few hundred bucks a month. And so I say, "Come on. Where else can you get a business that has the upside potential that this does?"

You might stumble a bit out of the gate. In 1995, when I first started as a real estate agent, my coach said to me, "I want you to call 12 people daily, just 12 people." I remember literally shaking and sweating at my desk trying to get through the 12 calls. In hindsight, I see how foolish that seems now. But in 2013, when we reengineered this business, I had to create and learn a different script, a different role, a different structure, and it wasn't easy. I remember my son-in-law Zach starting out brand-new at the scripts, with no experience, sending me taped audio files of his calls that showed he had a long way to go until he mastered the job. Just ten months later, he had become an absolute machine with the scripts—it was his call that brought in the deal at the beginning of this chapter.

We are offering partnerships in which you'll have my team and me calling on prospects with you, which will shorten your learning curve dramatically and bridge the gap between brand new investor and master transaction engineer.

NO SUBSTITUTE FOR EXPERIENCE

Your prospects will look at our experience and credibility. For example, one of our JV Partners initiated a call with a man selling a beautiful, 4,000-square-foot, $525,000 Virginia home just blocks from the ocean. She had a decent conversation with the seller but felt a little unsure and told him the next step would be for him to speak with her senior partner—me. A few days later, I spent 20 minutes on the phone with the seller, who told me he was favoring our company over a national competitor because he had checked out our Better Business Bureau rating, testimonials, and track record and liked the fact that we had a family company. That's how credibility and experience can produce a five-figure payday.

In contrast, one of our JV Partners surprised us with continual inquiries. After each e-mail, my son would ask me, "Why are they changing the system? The system works for us." And so we had a very blunt talk with that partner to say, "I get it that you're nervous. I get it that you're not clear on how to deal with buyers, but just follow the exact system we're talking about, right down to using the exact e-mail response to a buyer that we give you, using the exact script on the phone system voice mails that we give you." We could see that the partner's second-guessing had been muddying up communications and driving away buyers. Not long after our talk, the partner made a successful first deal and received a Payday #1 check.

If I could outline an ideal path for new partners, it would begin with what I call an "initial foundational game-plan call" with me. We can put the lead-generation mechanisms in place to get the right number of leads from the right sources. We'll do your first few calls for you and send you the recordings. Then we'll start doing some three-way phone calls together or provide recordings of follow-up to your calls. At any time in the relationship with us as a JV Partner, if you feel stuck, nervous, unsure of your next sentence or scripts—anything whatsoever—you simply pull back and say, "You know what? I think I've got enough information. I'm going to have my senior partner give you a call." You always have that as a crutch at any stage of the business.

Finally, as part of this predictable game plan, you have our team actually paying for your first batch of leads that are going to be done right in your marketplace for you (depending upon which program you choose with us). So this path leads to, potentially, a deal in your first month, but again, managing expectations, it could take up to six months. And that's not so bad considering the size of the paydays we are talking about. Remember, our two higher-level JV programs actually have me traveling to your market and being at the homes with you. We guarantee deals as you learn.

TESTIMONIALS FROM . . .

An Office Visit

"Hey Chris, It was absolutely amazing to be part of your team for a day. It motivated me to push forward on my business and adopt many of the strategies we discussed. Nick, Kayla, and Zach were great, and now I understand why you are able to close so many deals on a monthly basis: you've got a rock-solid team!"

—Enis S.

Mastermind-Group Participants

"We have been in two Mastermind groups with Chris and have already registered for the next one coming up. The knowledge, support, and encouragement we receive from being a part of this group are truly invaluable and have helped us so much in our business. It's great to have the opportunity to talk with other people who are going through some of the same challenges and successes that we are, and it gives us a sense of camaraderie. Chris is amazing and answers our questions and gives us education and suggestions during our group discussions. . . . The expertise and guidance he provides is something you can't put a price on. We are also in Chris's one-on-one coaching and would highly recommend that as well. We just got four properties under contract in nine days thanks to Chris's help and support."

—Jeff and Tami S., Seattle, WA

A Speech to a Local Association

"Dear Chris, I very much appreciated your taking the time to make your presentation Thursday night. I'm sure it was the end of a very long day for you. The feedback I received indicated that you were clearly knowledgeable and in the real world doing the very deals you described. Your presentation maintained interest with stories, and there was good audience participation throughout. I feel the listeners had gained some insights into a way of doing real estate practiced by almost no one here in RI, and you made available some very valuable tools for implementing your strategies."

—Rick C., REREIG, Rhode Island

JV Partner on Mentorship

"I'm a social worker by training and have only a small amount of experience in real estate investment. Chris turned out to be the perfect mentor for me, as he takes me step-by-step through the many processes that he knows so well. Even my most basic questions are taken seriously, and I always feel like I'm getting traction and making headway week after week. I'm not floundering anymore by aimlessly and endlessly searching through real estate investment websites or other types of coaching that don't have anything to do with my goals. I now have solid plans and objectives that I am continuously meeting as long as I show up and do the work. Chris encourages me to take steps on my own when I am ready but is always there with a helping hand for when I'm unsure of what to do next. I would highly recommend coaching and mentoring with Chris Prefontaine, whether you

are a beginner or have many years in the field. He has a wealth of knowledge to share and is always happy to impart it."

—Kate M., Connecticut

A Successful Home-Study Member

"I asked for and received a 10 percent down payment ($15,000). The monthly lease amount is $1,400, and the contract is for two years. I bought this house originally to flip. I paid $75,000, and I put in around $25,000 to fix it up. The purchase price is $149,900, so by the end of the deal, I will have made 50 grand over two years, plus 24 for the lease payments . . . over $83,000 in income all total. Not too bad! And all this while only accessing the membership area—super, super helpful!"

—Laurie T., Rhode Island

Joint-Venture Partners

"It has been a long haul, but thanks to your guidance, amazing patience, and continuous education efforts, I am now doing deals with sellers! I contracted with one yesterday and have another scheduled for this week. A third just called me last evening and is eager to sell to me as soon as possible. And I already have two scheduled for September. I am one of the many who have spent tens of thousands of dollars over the past year searching elsewhere for the right mentor and system to enable me to invest and profit in the real estate field. My total success prior to connecting with you was exactly one wholesale deal that netted $4,000. The one we bought Saturday (thanks for being available on the phone for us—those live calls help a lot!) has a monthly spread (Payday #2) of $305, a back end of approximately $29,000 (Payday

#3) and an up-front of $10,000 (Payday #1). That's $49,980 with all three Paydays—yeah! I bless the day I saw your video that encouraged me to just sign up for membership a month at a time. Within two months, I saw the value of committing to the JV program and have never looked back. I am retired and lost a lot of money in the stock market . . . twice! This field is so much more hands-on than the market, and as you have taught and demonstrated to me frequently through your own investing success, well within my ability to succeed and regain my former lifestyle on my own terms. Further, as a JV Partner, I have the incredible availability and support of you and your family with all aspects of each deal and its variables. The weekly mastermind calls, the videos and audios on the website, and the very complete and well-written transaction documents, as well as marketing and follow-up documents, make the actual processes crystal clear. I am particularly grateful for your willingness to deal with non-technical aspects of our partnership and the business, resulting in newfound confidence with seller calls (big deal!), efficiency, and creativity. I've gone from being a glorified assistant for myself, practicing "creative procrastination," to getting out there and making the necessary calls and contacts to create deals. It makes this fun and really quite exciting!"

—Claudia D., Arizona

QLS Home Study Video Course

"I highly recommend QLS Home Study Video Course for anyone who wants to get into real estate investing with little or no money. I have seen many other trainings that offer the same thing but are completely not realistic. Chris Prefontaine's no-

nonsense, no-holding-back strategies are why I joined his team as a JV partner in January 2017. There is no mentor or coach that will work side by side with you out the gates and has a real interest in helping you close deals. After watching QLS Home Study Video Course, you will see Chris's experience and sincerity with wanting to close deals with you. My wife has even left her high-level tech job to join me full time. We absolutely love our decision and look forward to a long profitable relationship with Chris and his team. Thank you Chris!"

—Gabriel Haney

" purchased QLS back in November. I have to say I was a bit skeptical. I have been in real estate since 1992, but the course is packed with information that you can use today to purchase properties with little or no money out of pocket, with no credit and more importantly, generate huge profits. Chris and his team are not just teaching a course, they do this every day and they know their stuff. If you are willing to put forth the effort and follow what they teach, you will be successful."

—Dave Mulvaney

"Hi my name is Sal, I was an investor in the good old days of 2004-2007 until everything blew up. I took a break for a while until now. I have dozens of books, courses, webinars, videos, and been to many bootcamp seminars. I have spent tens of thousands. When I saw Chris and how he ran his real estate investing business I knew that he had what I needed to get back on my feet and into the investing business again. His QLS course is spot on. He breaks down exactly what you need to succeed and how the terms investing really works step by step. I have a lot of courses

and his by far surpasses all of them. If you are a new investor and want to learn the true way of buying and selling on terms then this course is a must watch. If you are an old-time investor like I was, then this will add to your ways of investing and teach you new techniques. But what is even better is how he shows you a system to do multiple deals and not get stuck doing one at a time. I just signed up as a JV partner and I have accomplished more in one month then I have tried doing it my old way in the last nine months. Thanks Chris and team! looking forward to doing many many deals together."

—Sal B.

conclusion

By having regimented programs that allow new investors to take one logical step at a time to become a master transaction engineer, we hope we have made it easier for those who are ready to take the next step into a rewarding business of making deals on YOUR TERMS. It's a business in which you can be a hero to sellers and buyers who have no other recourse and earn astronomical returns without risking your own money. We've been up-front in this book about the "Yeah, buts" that we hear from those who are hesitant about our business model and how we've dealt with everything that can or does go wrong. We've offered to lock arms with you and walk you through your first deals, with guaranteed results.

If you have all the information you need already, go to Smart-RealEstateCoach.com, pick your program, or apply for JV Partnership consideration, and get ready to start. As a bonus for your having read this far, I am offering you a free, 15-minute one-on-one strategy call with me. Remember earlier in the book I talked about relaxing in Grand Cayman. I'll eventually be there a lot more—so visit our website to schedule your call soon.

If you are still unsure which of our programs is right for you, let me walk you through why you might choose the "middle-of-the-road" Joint-Venture Partnership program that you'll see when you visit the site. It's called the 5-Day Immersion Program. We will come to your marketplace for at least five days, with appointments we have made in advance to visit sellers with you. Our field agents and virtual assistants will work in your area to guarantee a minimum of 50 leads, from which we guarantee we can partner with you to close deals that we will help you process from start to finish. That includes any and all necessary legal forms and actually working it right through to the collecting of the check at the table with the attorney we will help you find.

You will get 12 full months of membership on our site, plus coaching. Your website will be done for you, and it will include every Buyer and Seller Q&A video that we've developed over the years. You'll also get the complete "Quantum-Leap System Home-Study Video Course." You can participate in our mastermind groups and one-hour weekly brainstorming calls, when they run. Even after our visit, we're still going to partner on the next three through ten deals with you and have our buyer specialist get involved and show you exactly how to close with every single buyer. We've structured it as a win-win, where we know it's worth our time and money, but at the end of the ten deals in which we share profits, you can be off on your own or use our coaching and mastermind groups as needed. That's the 5-Day Immersion Program. There are higher levels and lower levels of Joint-Venture Programs. At this level you will also attend our exclusive events, the yearly mastermind session for partners only, and our yearly JV dinner—all free.

In every market around the country, there are buyers and sellers exactly like those I have introduced throughout this book just waiting for you to make a deal with them, and I guarantee you can do it on YOUR TERMS.

OMB NO. 2502-0265

A.	B. TYPE OF LOAN:				
U.S. DEPARTMENT OF HOUSING & DEVELOPMENT **SETTLEMENT STATEMENT**	1. ☐ FHA	2. ☐ FmHA	3. ☐ CONV. UNINS.	4. ☐ VA	5. ☐ CONV. INS.
	6. FILE NUMBER: 25095.10001			7. LOAN NUMBER:	
	8. MORTGAGE INS CASE NUMBER:				

C. NOTE: This form is furnished to give you a statement of actual settlement costs. Amounts paid to and by the settlement agent are shown. Items marked "[POC]" were paid outside the closing; they are shown here for informational purposes and are not included in the totals.
1.0 3/98 (IRASPROPERTY:174FRANCIS.PFD/25095.10001/1)

D. NAME AND ADDRESS OF BORROWER:	E. NAME AND ADDRESS OF SELLER:	F. NAME AND ADDRESS OF LENDER:
▬▬▬▬▬	▬▬▬▬▬	
G. PROPERTY LOCATION:	H. SETTLEMENT AGENT:	I. SETTLEMENT DATE:
▬▬▬▬▬	▬▬▬▬▬ PLACE OF SETTLEMENT ▬▬▬▬▬	June 2, 2016

J. SUMMARY OF BORROWER'S TRANSACTION		K. SUMMARY OF SELLER'S TRANSACTION	
100. GROSS AMOUNT DUE FROM BORROWER:		**400. GROSS AMOUNT DUE TO SELLER:**	
101. Contract Sales Price	280,000.00	401. Contract Sales Price	280,000.00
102. Personal Property		402. Personal Property	
103. Settlement Charges to Borrower (Line 1400)	2,282.00	403.	
104.		404.	
105.		405.	
Adjustments For Items Paid By Seller in advance		*Adjustments For Items Paid By Seller in advance*	
106. City/Town Taxes to		406. City/Town Taxes to	
107. Sewer/Taxes to		407. Sewer/Taxes to	
108. Assessments to		408. Assessments to	
109.		409.	
110.		410.	
111.		411.	
112.		412.	
120. GROSS AMOUNT DUE FROM BORROWER	282,282.00	*420. GROSS AMOUNT DUE TO SELLER*	280,000.00
200. AMOUNTS PAID BY OR IN BEHALF OF BORROWER:		**500. REDUCTIONS IN AMOUNT DUE TO SELLER:**	
201. Deposit or earnest money	1,000.00	501. Excess Deposit (See Instructions)	
202. Principal Amount of New Loan(s)		502. Settlement Charges to Seller (Line 1400)	1,343.00
203. Existing loan(s) taken subject to		503. Existing loan(s) taken subject to	
204.		504. Payoff First Mortgage	
205.		505. Payoff Second Mortgage	
206. Seller Financing	275,800.00	506. Seller Financing	275,800.00
207.		507. (Deposit disb. as proceeds)	
208. 1A - Sec$750/Rent 6/3-6/30	1,380.00	508. 1A - Sec$750/Rent 6/3-6/30	1,380.00
209. 1B - Sec$700/Rent 4 mo.	3,500.00	509. 1B - Sec$700/Rent 4 mo.	3,500.00
Adjustments For Items Unpaid By Seller		*Adjustments For Items Unpaid By Seller*	
210. City/Town Taxes 01/01/16 to 06/02/16	2,236.08	510. City/Town Taxes 01/01/16 to 06/02/16	2,236.08
211. Sewer/Taxes to		511. Sewer/Taxes to	
212. Assessments to		512. Assessments to	
213. 2A - Security	750.00	513. 2A - Security	750.00
214. 2A - Rent 6/3-6/30	675.00	514. 2A - Rent 6/3-6/30	675.00
215. 2B - Security	750.00	515. 2B - Security	750.00
216. 2B - Rent 6/3 - 6/30	675.00	516. 2B - Rent 6/3 - 6/30	675.00
217. 3A - Security and Last	1,550.00	517. 3A - Security and Last	1,550.00
218. 3A - Rent 6/3 - 6/30	697.50	518. 3A - Rent 6/3 - 6/30	697.50
219. 3B - Rent 6/3 - 6/30	405.00	519. 3B - Rent 6/3 - 6/30	405.00
220. TOTAL PAID BY/FOR BORROWER	289,418.58	*520. TOTAL REDUCTION AMOUNT DUE SELLER*	289,761.58
300. CASH AT SETTLEMENT FROM/TO BORROWER:		**600. CASH AT SETTLEMENT TO/FROM SELLER:**	
301. Gross Amount Due From Borrower (Line 120)	282,282.00	601. Gross Amount Due To Seller (Line 420)	280,000.00
302. Less Amount Paid By/For Borrower (Line 220)	(289,418.58)	602. Less Reductions Due Seller (Line 520)	(289,761.58)
303. CASH (FROM) (X TO) BORROWER	7,136.58	*603. CASH (TO) (X FROM) SELLER*	9,761.58

The undersigned hereby acknowledge receipt of a completed copy of pages 1&2 of this statement & any attachments referred to herein.

Borrower ▬▬▬▬▬   Seller ▬▬▬▬▬

303. CASH TO BORROWER   7,136.58

DAILY DISCIPLINES: THE POWER OF ONE

Month: _____

	Frequency	Goal	1	2	3	4	5	6	7	8	9	10	11	12	13	14	15	16	17	18	19	20	21	22	23	24	25	26	27	28	29	30	31	Actual
New Contracts/200 monthly																																		
FSBOS																																		
Expireds																																		
Recognize Someone																																		
Yoga/Meditate 4x																																		
Cardio																																		
Run 3x																																		
Stomach 4x																																		

For all Forms, Agreements,
Checklists and more, see
www.smartrealestatecoach.com
Resource Area.

what do i do next?

www.SmartRealEstateCoach.com

- Free ebook: Eat that Sandwich - Creating Cash Flow Now, Cash Flow Monthly & Large Wealth with Sandwich Leases.
- Free Marketing Report: Gather Your Nuts - How to Generate Unlimited Leads
- Free Live Webinar

Quantum Leap Systems Home Study Video Course
*** Most Popular ***

- Monthly and yearly membership
- Mastermind Group Coaching Sessions
- One-on-one private consulting

Joint Venture Partnership Programs

- JV Club Level
- JV Starter
- JV On-Site Immersion
- JV High 6-Figure Income, Protected Area & Coaching Opportunities

For your free 15-minute strategy call as a reader of
Real Estate On Your Terms
email: Support@smartrealestatecoach.com
and include the subject line: On Your Terms-Strategy Call